TRIGGER FINGERS

TRIGGER
FINGERS

PERSONAL BRANDING
THROUGH STORYTELLING

ADAM RODRICKS

IGUANA

Publisher: Meghan Behse
Editor: Johanna Petronella Leigh
Front cover design: aksaramantra

ISBN 978-1-77180-558-2 (paperback)
ISBN 978-1-77180-559-9 (epub)

This is an original print edition of *Trigger Fingers: Personal
Branding through Storytelling.*

For Janice, my mother, who gave me life
&
Amberlie, my wife, who makes mine worth living

"*Use what talents you possess; the woods would be very silent if no birds sang there except those that sang best.*" —Henry van Dyke

Contents

The Boy Who Fibbed

It was in the second grade that I first encountered the needles so sharp in my throat that I could barely swallow without tearing up.

"What does it feel like?" asked the school nurse over the hum of her office heater.

"Like I've swallowed a weedwhacker!"

"Don't be so dramatic—how about you give both the talking and the tall tales a break? The rest will do you good."

She placed two hands so firmly on my shoulders that they generated more of a shove than a guide out her door, and I was sent back to class such that my only concession was the first half of recess.

I sat alone in the dimly lit classroom while my teacher, Mr. Coady graded our first-ever essays, entitled "What I Want Most for Christmas." I watched as his red pen dove into each child's musings. As he finished and flipped them over, a sea of Cs and Ds came into my view. I hoped with each subsequent one that he had not yet reached my own.

Mr. Coady was a tough but fair man, an undercover nurturer although you'd never know it by his intimidating stature. His face rested in a scowl and furrowed brow by default, his bottom lip perpetually curled as if his mouth was filled with the most succulent morsel of a medium-rare steak. To this day, I am convinced that he is, in fact, the inventor of the resting bitch face.

I knew I had to do something to spare my essay a similar fate to my classmates', if it were not too late.

"You know, Mr. Coady," I managed out as a burning fire engulfed my throat.

"I think you're going to like my essay. It really taught me something about my faith…"

Shameful as it was, I sat in a Catholic school, and I knew what a Catholic teacher would want to hear.

"Mmm," Mr. Coady growled, without looking up. So I continued.

"All I want for Christmas is a gold pendant of Jesus. So He can be with me always! I'm sure a lot of my classmates asked for things like bikes and Game Boys, but to me, this was an assignment that was really about what we want in life, not just at Christmas."

I practically shouted the end of my false proclamation, half to assuage the pain coming from my gullet, and partially because he was paying me little-to-no attention as his red pen did the talking across each page.

"I really think you'll like it, I feel like I learned a lot…" but my words were drowned out by the bell signifying the end of break.

Mr. Coady stood up as his students flooded into his classroom in a tidal wave of tumult; he began passing out the marked assignments. Without words, I waited patiently as the entire pile was handed back. Finally, he extended the cone-like shape my pages made as he passed them back to me upside down. He made eye contact briefly, the general lack of amusement still fixed upon his face.

I turned it over to reveal an A grade that I did not deserve.

Excited and somewhat delirious, I raced home that afternoon to show my parents what I had achieved.

I held the paper in my hands high above my head, brandishing the top mark as if I were Rafiki presenting the new-born lion king of Pride Rock. My mother's silhouette observed it through my outstretched hands on the other side.

She looked from the paper in my arms to the fridge behind me, where my wish list to Santa hung with a Pluto magnet. I watched as her gaze darted back and forth between the two.

"This is very good, my son," she said in a measured tone.

"But you wrote about how badly you want a pendant of Jesus in your paper; meanwhile your Christmas list to Santa has 20 items, and it's not mentioned even once there. Adam, are you telling stories again?"

This was her nice way of asking if I had fibbed to get the grade. And while I would succumb to a momentary flash of shame as I was confronted with the truth, the rest of my tiny body consisted solely of strep throat and pride.

For the first time in my life, I caught a taste of successfully marketing myself.

***

I assure you the man who writes these words now is far less flippant in how he sells himself. And while I hesitated to begin with a story that holds such negative connotations in this first foray into marketing oneself, it is a testament to the authenticity I pledged to put into each and every anecdote: unabashed and transparent accounts of what's made me both a storyteller and a man who is personal-brand obsessed. This is my superhero origin story, if you strip away the otherworldly abilities and substitute the general shittiness of an eight-year-old for a radioactive spider bite.

Who I am is an international-award-winning social media marketer who has transformed "word of mouth" into a world of mouth for some of the world's biggest brands and earned the title of "Canada's Top Social Media Strategist" by the Speakers Bureau of Canada.

For seven years, I've led Digital and Social at one of Canada's largest professional services firms. I teach personal branding fundamentals at a Toronto-based college, and I serve on the Program Advisory Board for Digital Engagement Strategy at another post-secondary institution in my home province of Ontario. The cross-section of education and storytelling has always been where I do my best work.

And I've been fortunate enough that this work has been featured on television, radio and on stages for thousands of people, most notably at Collision Conference, the largest technology show in the entire world. And it was coming off those stages that people would approach to tell me that it was never the lessons that resonated with them so much as the stories. And now I've written them all down so that, once and for all, these stories can leave my lips, and they can cease being mine and become ours.

After all, at face value these stories may seem like they are about me, but they're really about you: what you can extract, what you can then apply to your own personal brand and what you can avoid in your pursuit of establishing the absolute best representation of who you are and what you do.

I've always found that in Digital, we fixate far too much on future-proofing, forecasting and iterating for further success, when really, much of what made me a marketer is entrenched in my past. So it is my hope that through these stories, you marry these lessons to your unique qualities and therein create a cosmic explosion of what is inherently you.

Speaking of the lessons behind these stories, they are, in fact, as basic as pumpkin spice lattes. You could learn them from a number of books so I'll be clear up front that what will stick from this book is not necessarily the lessons on personal branding so much as the way in which they were learned.

You see, the most effective books on branding share stories of transformation:

- Why you do what you do
- How you've used your knowledge and skills to help others
- How it made you and them feel

Trigger Fingers endeavours to do all three. Thank you for coming along on this journey with me. I assure you, it's my sole reason for writing this book, and although it's all I've wanted to do, I'll never try to convince you that it was ever at the top of my Christmas wish list.

Scars from Sin City

"When writing the story of your life, don't let anyone else hold the pen." —Unknown

A drunken loudmouth with double vision shouts "Hit me!" to the club bouncer instead of the blackjack dealer, and then it (quite literally) hits him: the Las Vegas Strip is home to some painful realities.

Sadly, I am no exception. I have my own "coming to terms" story from Nevada; I want to tell you the most hurtful thing anyone has ever said to me in my professional life.

CES 2013 — Every January, the most influential tech event in the world brings to Las Vegas an abundance of tech geeks and not nearly enough deodorant. I was fortunate to earn a spot among the 150,000 people attending as a roving reporter, scouring the show floors for the hottest in technology for the upcoming year. I landed with a film crew and a contingent of merchandising colleagues who used CES as an excellent opportunity to network with their clients in the industry.

Among the clients I was introduced to was a man named Paul. Paul was the personification of a turtle, down to his shell-like hump. His facial skin was wrinkled like genitalia, his brow perpetually furrowed, and he wore the chunkiest of bifocal glasses that accentuated some features while completely obscuring anything beyond the outer limits of his eyelids. What's worse, Paul smelled like milk.

No matter what time of day or night we saw him, it was as if Paul had just emerged from bathing in dairy. On the spectrum of smell, Paul fell firmly in that grey zone of mildly off-putting yet not quite repugnant. Nevertheless, Paul was a valued client and so he received preferential treatment from my company. This mostly came in the form of VIP access to venues with the film crew through the side entrances, away from the hour-long lines that plagued the general public. Occasionally, he'd watch the interviews I conducted; often he would just disappear altogether, and aside from his moo-juice musk, there was only one other thing I distinctly remember: Paul was a total fanboy for celebrities.

On the third day of CES, my entire trip was made by a last-minute call. There was a cancellation that landed me the biggest break of my life: interviewing my favourite rapper, Xzibit. A lifelong fan of albums like *Restless*, movies like *8 Mile* and shows like *Pimp My Ride*, I was positively giddy. I spent the entire night before poring over my laptop and channeling my inner Nardwuar "The Human Serviette," learning every detail about the hip-hop icon, the Monster headphones he was there promoting and anything of interest that could come up in the 90 seconds I had been given to shoot with him.

The next day, I took my mark next to Xzibit as the cameras got ready. I leaned over to give him a fist bump at the same time he reached out and shook my hand firmly. Not the greatest start.

"We're ready," shouted the director, and I took a few deep breaths, knowing I only had one shot at this. Standing off in the distance, the crew were nodding in encouragement. Paul was there too.

I refocused my gaze back on X only to find he was still answering an email or a text. For a second, I thought about it from his perspective. All day long he was expected to make small talk with people who cared more about distortion ratios and frequency ranges than they did about him ... Did any even ask how he was doing?

"X, it's a real honour for me to be here with you, and don't worry, I'm going to keep it real for this—I'm ... I'm not an actor with a record deal tryin' to play the part."

He stopped typing and looked up. "What?"

And I did something I haven't done since I was showering in the tenth grade: I rapped Xzibit lyrics out loud.

I was certain it sounded far better when my vocals were muffled by the steady stream of bathwater drowning out my prepubescent voice, but luckily it was enough to get a huge grin from him.

He chortled and looked over to his group standing slightly out of the shot, then gave me a hard dap. His ring clunked into my knuckle hard, but I was on such an adrenaline rush I couldn't feel anything below my shoulders.

To my relief, the interview went smashingly well, and when the crew had what they needed and Xzibit was completely out of sight, they embraced me like I'd just hit a walk off home run for seizing the moment.

Amidst the backslaps and high fives, the faint scent of spoiled milk announced Paul's arrival before I had even heard his voice.

"How'd you know all of that about Xzibit?" he asked me, matter-of-factly.

"Oh, I'm a fan," I said, still beaming and celebrating with the others.

"Right, right," he continued sarcastically. "You just recall rap lyrics from 20 years ago all the time? You sure you didn't internet-stalk him, that is *your thing*, right?"

The adrenaline coursing through me helped me to ignore how important Paul was and instead compelled me to say,

"I'm a social media manager, not an internet-stalker and—"

Before I could finish the rest of my response, Paul stepped in front of me.

"Don't tell me that's an actual job."

The crew, who had been tirelessly editing and uploading all our content to YouTube, perked up from a few feet away.

"This social media stuff is a craze, it'll pass. And when it does, people like you will be out of a job *you shouldn't even have in the first place.*"

For those who've been waiting for the dagger to drop, that was it—the most hurt I've ever been in my professional life. Paul didn't think I was underqualified, nor was he trying to get a rise out of me; he fundamentally believed social media was nothing but a passing fad, so I shouldn't have a job. I was worth nothing to him.

But as the comment cut through me, I remembered the bravery I had just shown in front of Xzibit; what challenge did this homogenized hater pose?

"So you don't believe in social media?"

"No."

"Your brand is nowhere on social media?"

"No! Don't need to b—"

But this time, it was me interrupting, calmly but confidently.

"Let's see."

They say sometimes when you're filled with rage, you can have an out-of-body experience as you fly off the handle. Thankfully, my handle stayed firmly grounded when I confronted Paul, the sour milkman.

I whipped out my phone and typed in the name of the company Paul had been proud to boast about owning this entire trip. We watched the spinning wheel, chugging at a snail's pace to load in the overcrowded halls of the convention. In an honest moment of recollection, I was repulsed; I wanted to be anywhere but shoulder to shoulder with this man, but he had just insulted me and the lovely people around me who were working so hard—the page finally loaded while the hotness filled my face.

As the words came into view, I quickly realized Paul was right about one thing—we found no owned properties, on any social media platform, anywhere on the internet.

Damn!

But what happens when you type something into a search engine? Does it ever fail to return results, or does it yield literally hundreds of millions of hits for your query?

Paul's face dropped from overt smugness to sheer horror at the top results of my Google search. I still remember those coveted top three positions to this day.

First page result: article with misinformation and accusations about Paul's brand, published by a smaller player in his industry (clearly an early adopter of the fake news movement).

Second result: an announcement of an award for Paul's brand, with zero traction and engagement on the page, because no community had been established to amplify it.

And last but perhaps most maddening of all: unanswered pages of genuine questions from would-be customers, with a zero-out-of-five rating next to the company's name.

Paul peered closer and read furiously as I pulled my phone away. I saw the desperation in his eyes as he followed the phone even after the screen shut off and it disappeared into my pocket.

"What was the last one? What was the last question that girl asked about us?" he demanded.

I let him stew for a second in silence, his desperation palpable to the crew he had just insulted. Then, deciding this was a colour I didn't look good in, I offered to meet him for a drink later and go over it in detail.

That evening, Paul met me in the lobby of the Flamingo and, along with his coat, he checked his ego at the door. And then, together, we learned a valuable lesson in business: when you don't own your story, you open the door for someone else to write it for you. And written it they had, unfavourably and extensively. The conversation online is forever unfolding, with or without our participation.

Paul returned from that trip with the openness to explore a social media strategy. His company ended up launching multiple social media properties in the next 12 months, and as of the time of writing, they were just recognized for an award in online customer service.

I'm genuinely happy for them. After all, there's no use crying over spilt milk.

***

DEVELOP YOUR PERSONAL BRANDING STATEMENT

Have you heard that your personal brand is what people say about you when you aren't in the room?

Well, what do you think they say?

Developing your personal branding statement is the first step in steering that conversation.

Your personal branding statement is succinct: a summary of 1–2 sentences of what you do and why the way you do it is unique. Best of all, you can leverage your personal branding statement in networking to ensure you have a strong opener to captivate your audience.

SO HOW DO YOU CREATE A PERSONAL BRANDING STATEMENT?

STEP 1: Use free-flow writing to list your skills, your areas of experience, your strengths and your aspirations.

STEP 2: Think of your audience: Where are you the happiest when doing the things on your list?

STEP 3: Fire up LinkedIn. Search for and find a few people in your industry. How do they describe themselves and what they do? Great! Now make sure you're saying something *different*.

STEP 4: Go back to your list from Step 1 and pull out those qualities, experiences or strengths that differentiate you and make you unique from others in your field.

STEP 5: Go back to Step 2 and think about who of these people you would want to hire you. Don't overcomplicate it: you can simply narrow it down to a specific industry, location or even job title.

STEP 6: Do some simple math. Add your unique quality from Step 4 to your answer from Step 5. E.g.: "I do social media for companies in the insurance industry."

STEP 7: Refine your statement to make sure it's easily understandable and memorable. Instead of saying "*I do social media for companies in the insurance industry,*" you could say, "*I build communities that help others plan for the uncertainties in their future.*" And then continue to refine as needed.

Some examples of great personal branding statements include:

I help clients improve their company image and create websites with aesthetically pleasing and efficient interfaces. In doing so, I've increased company leads by 19%–154%.

I help companies with waste management and profit maximization. I do this by analyzing their facilities and processes to cut costs and develop more efficient practices.

Let's build great brands together.

Do you want to improve leads and traffic by up to 94%?

By organizing your time, you can organize your life.

I make big changes in small businesses.

Key Takeaway:	Lessons Learned:
Write your story or someone else will.	- The conversation online is going to happen with or without you. - Be authentic, even if doing so is uncomfortable. - There's no substitute in this world for hard work.

Questions to ask yourself about your personal brand:

- o   Do I know what's being said about me or my brand when I'm not in the conversation?
- o   Am I contributing to the conversation about myself online?
    - ▪   If not, who is?

Action Steps:

Artificial Intelligence

"Be yourself. Everyone else is already taken."
—Unknown

Is there anything quite as repulsive as trade-show food?

I weighed my options carefully, deciding between the risk of ingesting my breakfast bagel or just leaving it somewhere. I opted for the latter on my way through the auditorium doors for the next panel. At large convention shows, the ability to fill seats is usually derived from session titles that promise to be downright life changing. This track was no different. Aside from the fact I had willfully drunk the Kool-Aid, it was a panel discussion featuring one of my favourite pundits in the industry.

We'll call her Laney (after the main character of the 1999 American teen romantic comedy film *She's All That*) for the purpose of this story.

I took my place near the back of the hall and surveyed the room. I quickly checked Laney's Twitter account. Yes! She was here. She had moments ago arrived on the red-eye, and her last tweet came mere hours before, from a keynote in Berlin. The feelings of adoration and admiration for this woman who had seemingly hacked the 24-hour clock swelled within me as the lights went down.

The panel took their places on stage; a trumpet-backed walk-out song blasted through the auditorium as Laney came into focus and waved. She was dripping with excellence. Every bit of her appearance was polished, powerful but warm. I immediately snapped a picture for the tweet I hoped would catch her attention for a second, maybe getting a "like" if I was really on my game by adding one of those punchy, poignant pull quotes she was known for.

Laney was someone I respected for her expertise, her courageous commentary and her ability to seemingly manipulate time: she was the CEO of her own company, an up-and-coming investor in some very progressive biotechnology solutions, a best-selling author and a mother of three. She was the digital equivalent of a rock star Laney Gaga, if you will.

Touted as a visionary and an approachable leader, Laney was living proof that there was no substitute in this world for hard work. Simply being in her audience was making me want to get back to my computer.

Laney's session was as riveting as ever. She dropped statistic after statistic, pulling from a seemingly limitless repository in her mind to the exaltation of everyone in the crowd; she was every bit as insightful as I remembered from reading her work. Finally, her panel came to a close, and the moderator warned that, due to the incredible discussion on stage, there would only be time for one question to Laney.

A young lady immediately shot up and beckoned the microphone to her. She asked a simple but eloquent question about Laney's views on artificial intelligence, particularly what it would do to our existing jobs.

And Laney wasted no time launching into a gospel, one you could tell she cared deeply about. With as much passion as one can muster, she began to give us all a well-substantiated verbal essay on why A.I. would create *more* jobs than it would abolish. And although Laney spoke confidently and knowledgeably, you could see the silhouette of heads start swivelling, the whispers mounting to an audible hiss.

She looked around quizzically; it dawned on me that she may not even understand what was happening—she had lost the room for the first time in her career.

"But Laney—?"

She fidgeted with the microphone, waiting with pursed lips.

"You're always tweeting about how A.I. needs to be regulated—you backed that open letter on the need for stricter digital laws. What changed?"

The audience's murmurs mounted to a consistent hum.

The looks on the faces near me resembled that of a person hearing "I'm not pregnant" in response to the congratulations they've just offered. The cringe was palpable.

The answer to this young woman's rhetorical question had become clear to me: what changed from Laney's tweets to Laney's stance on stage was simply the author.

It was now painfully obvious to everyone in the room that Laney had a ghostwriter online. They "kept the lights on" so seamlessly and successfully that Laney had become known for those views and beliefs; all the while, she was doing the slew of other important things she was known for and believing something else entirely.

And as that doubt crept in, out the window flew the trust.

The lack of consistency between her online brand and her in-person brand was now as front and centre on that stage as the spotlight that illuminated the beads of sweat showing on her perfect brow.

She tiptoed around the rest of her response before swiftly exiting the stage to strained applause.

Disappointed to downright angry comments filled the air as we hurriedly emptied into the main hall again. Clearly, this discrepancy in Laney's stance caused trust in her brand to waver. For me personally, it was completely shattered.

What was deadliest about this decline? It was silent.

There was no booing. No one threw tomatoes, and the "Caps Lock" button on her fans' keyboards remained untouched in most of the comments on her posts thereafter. But in the days and weeks that followed, whenever I saw one of her messages pop up, I thought … *Is this her? Does she even feel this way?*

If I had wanted the opinion of her staff, I'd have followed their accounts for their unique perspectives. But I followed Laney for *her* insights, and if I wasn't getting that…

I stopped following her on every platform shortly after.

Clearly, others felt the same as her numbers plateaued then plummeted. What happened to her brand after that, I couldn't really tell you. Even when our paths crossed again and she had another session at a conference I attended, I'd made up my mind that my time would be better spent elsewhere.

If you'd told me I'd leave the auditorium feeling sick to my stomach that day, I'd have blamed the breakfast bagel. But there was something even more nauseating about the truth coming to light. Much like *The Wizard of Oz*, when the curtain fell on Laney, the tricks were exposed, and it was far from magical.

So what is the cost of shortcuts when you gamble with your integrity? It's trust.

Authenticity over everything.

***

"How to Actively Listen" Activity:

LISTENER AND TALKER ACTIVITY

The "Listener and Talker" activity is a great way to practice active listening. It only takes two people and can be done in five minutes.

STEP 1: Divide yourselves into pairs.

STEP 2: Assign one partner to the "talker" role and the other to the "listener" role.

TASK: The talker's job is to describe what they want from a vacation *without* specifying a destination. The listener's job is to listen attentively to what is being said (and what is not being said) and to demonstrate their listening through their behaviour.

STEP 3: After a few minutes of active listening, the listener should summarize the three main criteria the talker is considering when it comes to enjoying their vacation. Finally, the listener should try to *sell* the talker on a destination for their vacation.

STEP 4: After a quick debrief on how well the listener listened, the two should switch roles and try the exercise from the other's perspective.

This exercise gives each participant a chance to practice talking about their wants and needs, as well as an opportunity to engage in active listening and use the knowledge they gained to understand and relate to the speaker.

Best of all, you may get your next vacation destination out of it!

Key Takeaway:	Lessons Learned:
Authenticity over EVERYTHING.	- If it sounds too good to be true, it probably is. - The cost of being fake is the loss of trust. - If your audience becomes critical of the validity of your statements, they aren't listening to your brand's value proposition.

Questions to ask yourself about your personal brand:

☐ Is there anything about my approach that is disingenuous?

☐ Am I looking for efficiencies or cutting corners?

☐ Am I communicating transparently?

Action Steps:

The Starlit Letter

*"Your impact on the world is significant whether
or not you are aware of it, and even whether or
not you desire it."* —Gary Zukav

In seventh grade, Jessica Sitter passed a note down the row of
desks that eventually got to me and confirmed that she didn't
want to be my girlfriend. As much as that stung, it wasn't
even close to the worst letter I've ever received. Let me tell
you about that one.

I started writing at the age of 17 on a blog I created.

My shtick? Ranting and raving about the video games
that were worth our hard-earned money.

The approach was bland and repetitive, and I abused
semicolons like other forms of punctuation simply didn't
exist; some things never change.

Somehow, despite this sapped formula, I amassed a
following of 10,000 subscribers over the course of my first
two years of blogging. Everything changed around that
time. I started receiving emails from publishers, asking if

I'd like a review copy of their game before it was released. Did I mention they'd send the game for free? Seventeen-year-old me jumped for joy. Eventually, the games would come with an offer to place advertisements on my site in exchange for payments based on the referral traffic I generated. When I obliged, a cheque would soon follow in the mail.

Receiving physical cheques via snail mail may sound like the most bizarre part of that whole transaction, but in the year 2005, "online advertising" was a foreign concept to me and more importantly, a source of income when I needed it most.

So I sold my soul to the devil in banner-ad form, and two things started to happen:

#1. My review integrity started to drop because I felt terrible about scoring games poorly after they had so generously sent me a copy, and

#2. My blog comprised more ads than words.

The writing was on the wall—a lack of authenticity coupled with a poor user experience. You didn't need to study business to know that things were quickly headed in the wrong direction. And soon they did.

I thought about what I might be able to do to quell the fall from grace and settled on the only thing I felt was true to my brand and doable on my (renewed) shoe-string budget: hard-hitting journalism.

For months, readers had been asking me to investigate some suspicious surcharges that would appear on their receipts when they bought video game consoles at a particular Canadian retail store. At the register when they completed the transaction, the total amount would magically jump when an additional line item would appear on the bill listing a surcharge of five dollars that said, "Environment Disposal Fee." It seemed off because customers weren't "disposing" of anything.

I called the store, and the manager referred me to their head office. I called every day but got nowhere.

I called the console manufacturer and racked up some nasty long-distance charges, but alas that yielded little either.

In desperation, I called a series of government departments focused on environmental protection, climate change— anyone who would speak to me. But in true Canadian fashion, all I heard was "sorry" before a dial tone, and yet again I'd be left in the dark with nothing.

Well, not *nothing*. Readers were loving the investigative format.

Views of my blog and shares of my articles had skyrocketed. I was back, baby! Ad revenue hit an all-time high, and the strut to the mailbox once again became a part of my weekly ritual so I could extract those sweet, sweet ad cheques.

The next Friday night, I returned from school fairly late but certain I had aced one of my last-ever finals. For the first time in a long while, I felt in control.

Underneath the night sky, I walked to the mailbox and spotted a shooting star but nothing in particular came to mind. I pulled out that week's cheques. But instead of a stub falling out, it was a full-length letter. *Fan mail?* I thought, but it was too dark to make out, so I stepped under a street light.

My heart sank through my stomach, then my jaw joined it firmly on the floor.

This was no fan mail; this was an overly verbose, lawyer-written, consequence-infused condemnation, more colloquially referred to as a cease and desist. And all I can say about the penalty amount for failing to comply ... it featured a lot of zeroes.

I sped home, my heart beating so fast that I could see the accelerated rhythm on my shirt as I panicked over what to do. A minute ago, the prospect of a few dollars had brought me excitement, and now I was facing a fine so large it could be a down payment. All for some silly questions on a blog written by a kid hoping to save a few bucks? And this was happening mere weeks before graduation. Was I even going to be employable anymore? Was my degree all for nothing? Shrouded in darkness, I pinched and poked at myself hoping to wake up only to look down in the light and see specks of blood congealed under my fingernails. There was no waking up from this; I had to take action!

Immediately, I began deleting whatever I could find of myself online. Years of hard work dumped with a flurry of left and right clicks without so much as a second thought. I began to cry. Warm tears drenched my face as I thought about what I was going to tell my parents.

And then, I made the decision to be done with it all. I went dark completely. I put the muzzle on my online persona for the first and only time in my life. And I waited...

The next few weeks were agony; every ring of the phone or knock at the door induced a cold sweat all over. I walked on a sea of eggshells through my life in what would have otherwise been an exciting milestone: the brink of graduation. I went from habitually checking my mail to dreading the sight of that mailbox, praying that everyone would forget and leave me alone, that they wouldn't fine me or charge me, or worse.

Then one day, the phone did ring from an unknown number.

My stomach somersaulted as I picked up.

"Hi, is this Adam? The video game blog guy?"

An intense heat crawled up my neck and engulfed my ears as I hesitantly confirmed—ready for my fate.

"I'm a recruiter—we love what you've done with your community building, and we wanted to know if you'd come in to talk about an exciting new role we're hiring for."

"I haven't… What role? I haven't applied for anything," I said. "I did have a blog, but it's been deleted for months, and I haven't sent you a resume, there must be some mistake."

"Right, a lot of the links on Twitter were dead, but the discussions there were fantastic, so much so that we thought we'd reach out to you based on the strength of your portfolio…"

"My … portfolio?"

Never before had I considered what I was doing as "building a portfolio" that could provide anything beyond getting the odd free game. But here was this recruiter saying I had one that consisted of a thoughtful approach to content and promotion and asking if next Thursday afternoon would work with my busy schedule.

Astonished and humbled, I accepted. Three weeks later, I started working at Staples Canada, where I would start my (formal) career in the industry as the company's first dedicated resource to social media and community.

Two aspects of this ordeal stay with me to this day. The first is a warning—especially if you subscribe to the mentality that your life is an open book—ensure that you make present-day decisions that in the future you will not regret. What you create online lives in perpetuity (even when you think you've deleted it, as in my case).

The second lesson is that the first lesson isn't necessarily a bad thing. If it wasn't for my passion, consistently writing, committedly promoting my work, and the community I had built up, a recruiter would have never found my "portfolio." Your impact can be felt long after you've stopped talking.

With that in mind, what will you say?

Key Takeaway:	Lessons Learned:
The impact of your words is felt long after you finish talking.	- Trading ad revenue for authenticity leaves your brand shortchanged. - Once online, forever online: publish deliberately.

Questions to ask yourself about your personal brand:

- ☐ Am I saying this to elicit a reaction or because it needs to be said?
- ☐ How is the user experience? Would I enjoy it if I were a member of my audience?
- ☐ With this comment or post, am I building the type of brand I want?

Action Steps:

Before publishing anything online, try the *New York Times* test:

> The content you are about to post is not going on social media, but instead it's being published on the front page of tomorrow's the *New York Times*, next to your full name and picture.
>
> How would that make you feel? How would your boss react? Your mother?

If you think "great! This would be incredible exposure for my brand" then go ahead and hit "Enter."

However, if you feel any type of apprehension about how you'll be perceived or portrayed, consider reworking that piece of content until it's something you are proud of, regardless of who sees it.

Salt Stain on the Wound

"Instinct's the iron skeleton under all our ideas of free will." —Stephen King

The only similarity between me and a superhero is that on more than one occasion, my bright-red undergarments have also been visible, protruding from my pantaloons. When I was growing up in the late nineties in Scarborough, Ontario, it was the trend to sag one's pants, but I assure you it's neither stylish nor intentional when I do it.

As I was saying, I am no Batman, but on exactly one occasion in my life I have had the chance to feel like I made a difference when disaster struck.

It was the winter of 2018 on a particularly miserable Tuesday evening. Traffic in Toronto regularly moves at a crawl, but on this day it was made even worse by the absolute pounding of sleet and snow the city received. I arrived late at the local library to give a talk on digital branding. Not surprisingly, the theatre was almost completely empty. I wished I had stayed home too.

The library staff rushed forward and thanked me for braving the storm for them.

"The show must go on!" I exclaimed insincerely.

They continued with the setup, and I took to the washroom to wipe the salt stains off my pants. In Toronto, we use mounds of the stuff to ensure pedestrians don't slip on the icy walkways, but the drawback is that it absolutely decimates your clothing, particularly your pants and shoes. For someone about to take the stage and discuss putting your best *foot* forward, I most certainly didn't look the part; I became increasingly nervous as bits of moistened paper towel broke apart, leaving remnants all over me, far more noticeable than the salt I was trying to wash off.

We waited for more people but eventually realized that these scattered few were all we'd be getting as the weather continued to intensify outside. I was underwhelmed, but as I had so confidently spouted earlier, the show must go on.

It was an intimate group (that's what speakers say when we don't get the number of people we expect), and one of the advantages of a reduced crowd included more audience interaction. I've always found with smaller groups there is more opportunity to engage, which is particularly fun for someone who had delivered the exact same session a hundred times before.

So on this particular night, my direct eye contact bounced across the room from person to person, assessing candidates who may be up for some banter; a quick exchange would certainly help cut through the dreariness surrounding us.

It didn't take long for my eyes to rest on an elderly gentleman who looked back at me with palpable disdain. This is a regretfully common issue when speaking on the topic of new technology. A cynic in the audience—usually (but not always) of an older generation—would call it "bullshit," "a fad," "a farce," "a hoax" or "a passing craze"—that very technology I've built my career from. And when these rebuttals get hurled my way, peppered with antiquated skepticism, I can't help but hear it as "get off my lawn."

I smiled back at him, but his gaze didn't soften. Over the next few minutes, I found myself consciously skipping over him as I surveyed the room, meeting the eyes of everyone else, fearful for more negative reinforcement on a night where the limits of my tolerance had already been established in two very visible patterns of salt on my paper towel–caked trousers.

The evening trudged on, with perhaps a little more banter than usual and the occasional latecomer who burst in, covered in snow. After one lady apologized profusely for interrupting, I made a joke of it that landed quite well, and I mustered up the courage to look back at the elderly gentleman whose chagrin had not wavered in the slightest. In fact, his expressions of confusion and contempt were now supplemented by his arms crossed tightly over his chest and a slouch in his stature that looked awfully like he could fall asleep at any moment.

And then he did.

I watched as his head suddenly drooped, and with so few people in the audience, there was no one else close enough to take note. That's probably one aspect of being on stage that I'll never get used to—the incredibly unique perspective. In a room such as this, if I'm anywhere close to decently engaging, every eyeball in the room should be trained on me, with only my eyes staring back at you.

So when this elderly man folded in his chair, I was the only one who realized that it had happened. Immediately, my internal voice raced between what I had just seen, and the words that were simultaneously leaving my mouth to a live audience:

He's sleeping—he'll wake up if I shout the next line or two.

What a prick, who falls asleep like that? Just stay home if you're so tired.

But there are still a lot of people staring at you—stay focused now.

Seriously though, how rude is this asshole? He showed up, barely gave me a chance and now he's sleeping in my session.

… He is sleeping, isn't he?

The internal arguing did nothing to convince me. From the moment it happened, I felt my stomach somersaulting. Something was wrong.

I've learned a lot about addressing an audience in the five years since I started public speaking, but nothing that prepared me to interrupt my own talk, while on stage, as the one speaking.

What eventually fumbled out of my mouth I don't know. Truth be told I've suppressed it from my memory, so let me instead share how eloquently I remember it could have gone.

I walked back to the centre of the stage, thinking about the potential embarrassment of drawing attention to the man so bored by me that he literally could not stay conscious, and cringed at the idea of having him shaken awake for everyone to see firsthand how dull tonight's speaker was.

But what if he isn't sleeping…

I clapped my hands together, half-hoping to create a noise loud enough to jar him awake. Nothing. I knew I would have to break my own rule: the show must not go on. It must come to a screeching halt.

I broke from the middle of my sentence and caught the eye of one of the staff. She rose with every bit of urgency, expecting me to say that the teleprompter had stopped working, but instead I shared the very real concern that was in my mind's voice.

"Can you please check if he's ok?" I quivered.

I remember every head in the room cranking in unison to identify who I was talking about.

I remember the click-clack of the organizer's heels and the echoes of those shoes in the hall fading as she stopped next to him.

I remember when she put her hand, gently, on his shoulder and whispered directly into his ear, "Sir."

And I remember when the paramedics burst in to rush him away.

We left that night unfinished, wet, and fearful for the fate of a man none of us even knew. On the way home, I said a quick prayer, and committed to memory the three lessons I had just learned:

1.   Wet paper towels often make stains worse.
2.   To be engaging, you don't have to carry the conversation all by yourself.
3.   Always, always trust your gut.

Interrupting myself so publicly and drawing attention to a man who was sleeping in my audience still makes my hair stand on end when I think about it, but I'd rather suffer the embarrassment 10 times over than think about what would have happened had I ignored my gut feeling.

***

"I'm so sorry about the weather, the poor turnout and the ... circumstances," the library's organizer said when she called the next day.

"No problem at all—entirely out of your control. But speaking of, is he OK now?" I managed sheepishly.

"He's fine! He suffered a mild stroke, but they made it to the hospital in time. He's expected to make a full recovery."

"Oh, thank God," I said, in between the biggest sighs of relief my lungs could hold.

"You acted fast, Adam. So should we try that talk again? This time we'll book you in the spring so the turnout won't b—"

"Absolutely. The show must go on."

***

Presentation Activity:

TAKE A MUNDANE SLIDE AND TURN IT INTO THE STRONG POINT OF YOUR PRESENTATION:

Here are four ways you can take the most boring slide of your presentation and turn it into an opportunity to engage your audience.

- **A picture is worth a thousand words** – Consider reworking the slide to feature a picture and instead of paraphrasing the text on your slides, tell a story that the visual helps to drive home.

- **Information overload** – Have a slide that's too information dense? Remember the "rule of three"— people can remember THREE pieces of information really well, so what are your top three takeaways from this slide?
- **Rules of engagement** – Ask yourself how you can involve the audience by asking them questions:
  o If you sense audience members may be hesitant to speak, poll them using multiple choice or by a show of hands.
- **LOL** – The use of humour can lighten the mood and build a good rapport with your audience

And remember! Eye contact can help establish your stage presence and effectively deliver your point; the presentation will also feel more intimate, as if you are having a direct conversation.

Key Takeaway:	Lessons Learned:
Trust your gut instinct.	- Being punctual is the first impression you make before your first impression. - Don't assume the world is against you by default. - There are far worse consequences to not saying something than embarrassment.

Questions to ask yourself about your personal brand:

- ☐ If I speak up, what's the worst that could happen?
- ☐ Can infusing conversation into my presentation make the delivery more engaging?
- ☐ When I'm feeling uneasy or apprehensive in a situation, can I consciously evaluate why?

Action Step:

No Small Parts

"There are no small parts, only small actors."
—Konstantin Stanislavski

In high school, we were given a choice between taking either visual or dramatic arts. Because I suck something fierce at sketching anything beyond stick people, drama won by default.

One of the first things we did in class involved learning how to emote. In one assignment, we had to pull an emotion out of a hat and then do a one-minute improv on stage exhibiting that feeling for our peers to guess. I pulled the word "anger" and then proceeded to scream my lungs out for a minute straight.

I lost my voice, received a C+ grade, but worst of all, my teacher's critique referred to it as "a classic case of overacting."

For whatever reason, her critique struck a nerve at a vulnerable time in my adolescence when there was already stiff competition for most scarring feedback received.

I decided then and there that drama wasn't for me.

Fast forward to senior year, and the school play needed help. The production that year, *Bye Bye Birdie*, required an ensemble cast, and there weren't enough bodies to fill the roles. Hoping to do justice to the play, they tapped all students, current and former—even if they had a history of overacting.

Admittedly, I had a chip on my shoulder from when I was first approached. I thought, *To hell with them*. I'm pretty sure I even voiced that opinion out loud.

Besides, in a year I was preparing applications for post-secondary, every extracurricular I took on mattered even more—who was going to care if I took on a bit role in the school play? It was so insignificant and unimpressive. This was a firm no, an easy decision and one I made almost instantly.

Then the girl I liked signed up for the school play...

On the first day of rehearsals, all the new bit characters were introduced to the main cast. We were handed scripts, and because we were "bit" roles, our parts only consisted of stage directions. No lines, not even one.

Again, I weighed whether this was even going to be worth it; was I such an overactor that they couldn't even entrust me with a single line of dialogue?

I went through the motions, reluctantly. I'm not proud of this, but as my crush began to fade so did my interest in seeing this commitment through. I skipped rehearsals, I barely paid attention during read-throughs, and three weeks before we were set to open, I thought about making an excuse to back out completely.

Then, at one of the few rehearsals I did attend, we did a dry run of what the scene would look like. "Blocking" is what they called it. The lights would come up on a line of friars, all arranged in a row on the same side of a table, and the voluptuous main character would enter and entrance us all with a dance. Then, before the lights faded, one by one we'd each get "swallowed" by some unknown entity that would suck us under the table.

We went through the blocking, and when it was time for each of us to get sucked under the table, I was last. I watched as every single person before me clawed at the top of the table, then flailed and shouted a terribly unconvincing "*ahhh!*" as they disappeared. It was boring, it was bad, and I was mentally forging that doctor's note in my mind to get out of this already.

When my turn came, I didn't flail. I didn't claw. I didn't even want to be there. I thought about the accusation of overacting and out of spite, I did the exact same thing; I slammed my palms down on the table and let out a blood-curdling scream in the highest pitch I could, before dropping under the table.

The entire auditorium erupted. I assumed that my war cry was just what the contingent of undervalued bit actors had been waiting for to incite our rebellion.

From under the tablecloth, I could see the silhouettes of the other friars bouncing, and then it dawned on me: everyone was laughing. I emerged from under the table skirt, expecting to be scolded for yet again overacting, but I was quite wrong.

"Do that again," the director said.

By opening night, they had moved me to the front and centre of the table. For the next three nights straight, I put everything into my five seconds of fame—a look of panic and a high-pitched yelp you'd never dream could come out of a six-foot teenage boy on the right side of puberty. Despite me not uttering one word, it killed every time!

By the end of that week, the production wrapped, and the drama society hosted a dinner to thank all the bit role actors and actresses who had stepped up to make the play possible. A month earlier I had been ready to drop out, and now I was excited to see these people again.

At the dinner, several of the (real) actors came up to me and thanked me for taking part. I was amazed they'd even remembered given how much more substantial their contributions were to the play. Toward the end of the dinner, they handed out some awards. One was for the best bit role, and they called my name.

As I walked up to accept it, I saw the lead actors all looking on, clearly appreciative for my contribution, smiling and cheering me on. I saw my old drama teacher, also beaming, and I felt guilty that I was so ready to leave these people high and dry during my moments of shortsightedness.

If you subscribe to the thinking that all the world's a stage (and I do), then I want to share with you the lesson I learned in high school drama. Much like on stage, there are no small parts in life. Every moment—however fleeting or seemingly insignificant they may seem—is an opportunity to leave an impression. Make your mark on this world with every opportunity you get.

***

Constructive Feedback Activity:

HOW DO YOU GIVE CONSTRUCTIVE FEEDBACK?

The only thing harder than giving constructive feedback is receiving it. As you've read from my stories, I've been on both ends of constructive feedback.

So how do you position your criticism in a way that will resonate with the receiver?

Use the *BO-FID* method:

B is for Behaviour – Begin by describing the behaviour that led to this feedback: e.g., "You are interrupting me constantly" and avoid using judgemental statements that generalize like "you monopolize the conversation."

O is for Ownership – Use "I" to own your thoughts or feelings that are being expressed; don't speak in generalities like "people think you are mean" because this can convolute the validity of the statement.

F is for Feelings – In order for this feedback to be impactful, you need to include your real feelings about how the behaviour affected you. Don't misrepresent or downplay how you feel, or you run the risk of diluting the message you're communicating.

I is for Immediate – The most effective feedback is often given soon after the behaviour is exhibited, immediately if possible (but later if you need time to cool off before speaking; it's never a good idea to communicate from a place of anger).

D is for Direct – Don't involve other people or pass the blame. This is indirect feedback which is far less effective in implementing change.

Focus on how the **behaviour** made **you feel** and communicate those feelings as **directly** and **immediately** as you can.

This will help you get the most out of your tough conversations.

Key Takeaway:	Lessons Learned:
Make the most of the opportunities that you're given.	- Your word is an extension of your brand; be true to both. - See commitments through to the end. - The objective of constructive feedback is not to hurt you, but to make you better.

Questions to ask yourself about your personal brand:

- ☐ Is the tough feedback I was given valid? Is that why it hurts?
- ☐ Although my approach may have failed, are there elements I can carry forward for next time?
- ☐ Does quitting impact more people than me? If so, what are the long-term consequences of my short-term actions?

Action Steps:

Likes Aren't Free

*"It is true that integrity alone won't make you
a leader, but without integrity you will never
be one."* —Zig Ziglar

The two most shocking things I've ever been told to pay for
were sex and "likes" on social media. To my dismay, they
occurred hours apart on the same day.

Your first corporate work trip and your hundredth trip
are polar opposites. On the first trip, it resembles more of a
privilege than a responsibility. Everything about it feels like a
pleasure, from the plane ride to the per diem to the lovely sex
worker I shared a cab with to the hotel. Young and naïve, I
thought I was doing the company a huge favour by splitting
the transportation costs in half.

My sensitive nose alerted me from the second she eased
herself into the backseat; it was like being punched in the face
by her presence. Although her perfume was pungent, it was
the only overstated aspect of her. She was incredibly polished
and well-spoken, and I was grateful for the company. I was

green, clearly happier than I should be to have just landed from a four-hour flight to minus-25–degree weather.

In the movies, this is the part where the ambitious youth stares out the window as the skyline of the big city slowly comes into view over the horizon. Unfortunately for my story, I was in Edmonton, Alberta, in the pitch black of a cold November evening with a near opaque fog on the cab window obscuring anything worth a view.

With no sights to see, my fare-splitting comrade and I got into a conversation. Where are you from? How long are you in town for? The usual. She asked me if I knew anyone in the city. I confirmed that I didn't. When I asked her about work, she explained to me what "the girlfriend experience" was, and I tried my hardest best to keep the epiphany I'd just learned from showing on my face. I wish there was more to this part of the story, but the entire encounter was rather uneventful.

We arrived at the hotel, we wished each other well, I walked in and she carried on in the cab.

I went up to my room and began smelling my clothes for remnants of my new friend.

The next day, I was pitching a new client, a men's lifestyle publication, on what was supposed to be a fresh campaign idea to launch their YouTube channel. We were going to make a splash online by featuring real people—a concept called user-generated content. I had prepared meticulously and packed my best suit. My biggest mistake: not removing those clothes from my suitcase until the morning of; if you were keeping time, it was indeed amateur hour.

In my crumpled and rumpled but best attire, I strode into the meeting with an air of confidence. I had just read somewhere that confidence was the only thing that is as valuable to feign as it is to have, and this was going to carry me through to the finish line.

I began by talking about the fundamentals of user-generated content—or UGC for short. On the screen, I presented the words *Share a Coke* triumphantly, and spoke slowly as if I was half-anticipating being interrupted by the standing applause I thought I should receive.

But nothing…

Example after example fell flat until, finally, the clients in the room asked me if I would be willing to go to a local fast-food restaurant, buy a cup of scolding hot chili, and be filmed as I spilled it all over myself "accidentally."

"But, why?" I asked incredulously.

"We've seen all the stuff you're talking about, and we agree, using real people is the way to go. But your application of it is a little … pedestrian. It's not 'front page' good. What our followers respond to are the spectacles. Likes aren't free after all…"

This is the part I regret writing almost as much as I regretted saying, but I didn't retort with refusal, I reluctantly accepted.

"Awesome!" they exclaimed. And as one of the managers rapped me on the back in his excitement, I forced a smile onto my face as they talked about where to meet the crew the next day and what shots were critical to capture.

I went back to the hotel that evening, utterly defeated. I sat down at the hotel bar and I ordered the first of many drinks alone. As I downed one and then another, the backbone I wish I had exhibited in the boardroom started to appear, and with it, every clever retort I probably should have said. Instead, I had made a verbal commitment to ruin my second-best suit and possibly suffer third-degree burns in the process.

"Company?" the bartender asked me.

And I responded with the name of the company I worked for. "No, no," he laughed.

"Are you looking for company this evening?" and he slid a card across the table. In bright red letters, it said "Edmonton's Finest Girlfriend Experience."

"What? No, no!" I shot back. I took the card and slid it so hard across the bar that it flew off behind him.

"Alright, but ain't no shame in it," he said as he passed over my tab and went back to his other customers.

I remembered my new odoriferous friend and how nice it would be to talk to her right now, then snapped out of it. I paid my tab and went upstairs.

Still feeling the height of my liquid courage, I emailed the client and explained with as much sobriety and politeness I could muster that I wouldn't be able to produce the content we had agreed to. I apologized again in the morning by phone, and that afternoon I caught my scheduled flight back home to Toronto.

I wasn't fired, we didn't lose the account, there was no dramatic fallout, but I was never asked back by them again. There was no discernable aftermath from the ordeal, and yet that story has never left me.

I look back on it and I am disappointed in myself every time. Not because I failed the client, not because I seemed lonely enough to pay for company, but because I agreed to do something I wasn't comfortable with on social media, and that goes against everything I stand for—online and offline.

Likes may not be free, but you can never put a price on your integrity.

On my next trip to Alberta many years later, I proved to myself I had learned three very valuable lessons from the first time around: Be true to yourself, locate the ironing board and remember that every hotel room in North America comes equipped with a mini-bar free of judgement.

∗∗∗

Confidence-Booster Activity:

FAKE IT 'TIL YOU MAKE IT

It's been said that there is only one thing you can fake as effectively as you can have: confidence.

I'm here to tell you that the method works, especially to boost your confidence before you address an audience.

Here is my five-step process to fake it 'til you make it with presentations and public speaking:

STEP 1: Start by asking yourself what you would do if you felt confident in this situation. For starters, you'd probably conduct yourself in a similar way to when you're comfortable. You'd stand up straight, you'd lead with your chest out, your chin high, and you'd smile.

STEP 2: Once you've identified 2–3 answers to the question in Step 1, tell your body to direct your brain to emulate those behaviours. For now, we're just practicing at home, maybe in front of the bathroom mirror, but project the type of voice, body language and speech you envisioned from Step 1.

STEP 3: Before you get bogged down in memorizing lines or recounting statistics, define and focus on your goals of the presentation. If you're giving a wedding speech, you want everyone to know how much you love the happy couple. That's it. Start there, and keep your goals top of mind.

STEP 4: Now knowing what you *want* to do, and how you're supposed to look while doing it: don't act, just do. Practice projecting those behaviours to convey the message you identified in Step 3. Don't worry if it isn't long enough, or good enough. Once you get it down, you can easily expand upon it.

STEP 5: Repeat. The act of practicing the body language, the voice and the speech will inherently make you more comfortable delivering it. The words will sound familiar and to say them will become second nature with practice.

Before you know it, the confidence you've feigned will become the confidence you have. It's gained through experience and repetition so remember to practice, practice, practice.

Key Takeaway:	Lessons Learned:
Prioritize integrity when building brand (but really, all the time).	- Put the same level of effort into presenting yourself as your material. - "Fake it 'til you make it" can be an effective method to bolster your own confidence. - Be true to yourself or the brand you'll build may not be sustainable.

Questions to ask yourself about your personal brand:

☐ Have I considered every element of what I'm putting out there (content, appearance, preparations) so I can put my best foot forward?

☐ When I lack the confidence to speak, can I listen intently to ask smart questions instead?

☐ Am I being true to myself with my next move?

Action Steps:

My One-Man Show

"Short cuts make long delays." —J.R.R. Tolkien

Do you remember the point in your life when you started to get some real pocket money?

I don't remember it by age, but I can tell you it was around the same time that I started guarding my computer screen as closely as my social insurance number, those hormonal years when every young man would appreciate advance notice of having to stand up, especially when in the company of a pretty girl.

Most young men around this age had secured their first part-time job. If I'm being painfully honest, they'd also dated a fair bit and learned that treating a woman properly meant something more than what I'd do: offer to supersize her order of french fries.

I came to the stark realization I was broke about six weeks before my then-girlfriend's birthday. We were in a café, and her friend Dina opened a beautiful 14K-gold necklace and locket from her boyfriend. It opened up to display the word

"Forever" engraved on the inside cover next to a picture of them both.

Oh shit!

The bar had been set, and I had better rise to it lest I spend any more of my evenings on websites that promised me hot singles in my area.

I should point out that the pressure I felt was never amplified by her, but by the goings-on of the adolescent male mind, fully embracing every iota of insecurity and doubt that it's presented with, all wrapped up in a roller coaster of extreme emotions. Growing up was a trip.

As my girlfriend's birthday drew closer, I scraped together as many job applications as I could, and furiously submitted them to anywhere that was hiring. I received exactly two calls back. One was for a part-time shoe clerk in the mall starting the next month, and the other was handing out energy drinks on my school campus beginning immediately. The next day, I dawned the neon apron and started peddling liquid energy in a bottle.

I calculated that I needed to work 60 hours to buy the proper gift. I signed up for as many shifts as the promotional company would give me, and off to the races we went. By the end of this job, I had promised myself that I was either going to buy her love, or I was going to die trying.

From the very first day, I showed promise as both a salesman and a showman. It's often said that customers buy solutions to their internal problems, and framing energy drinks as a solution to fatigue was one way to do that. But it lacked pizzazz, so instead, I would chug a can and talk a mile-a-minute to demonstrate the abundance of energy it had given me. Think of Eminem rapping, but take away the rhythm, flow, lyricism and talent. It was comical, over the top and carnivalesque, but it worked.

Every 15 minutes or so, I'd gather a small crowd and begin speaking as fast as I could to show how much energy I had accumulated. I'd bounce all over the place, and by the end of my pitch, I was covered in a thin layer of sweat, but people stayed and listened. Moreover, intrigued by my antics, the energy drink cans started to move, so on I went. Even better, by the time most of my 12-hour shifts ended, I felt as if I had barely worked a minute.

On my way home, I'd think about all the things I could do next, my heart and mind still racing from my energy drink–induced high. I could meet up with my friends to smoke a joint and mellow out a bit, then do some homework, conduct a little research on "cheap gifts that look expensive" and still have something left in me for a little self-care time—you know, a late-night tussle with Russel the love muscle (or as Snoop Dogg would say: "Jizzle yo' wizzle 'til you expizzle"). Whatever I wanted, whenever I wanted—I had found a way to burn the candle at both ends. Life had been hacked.

Then one morning the following week, I woke up and I couldn't move my chest.

I struggled to turn over in my bed and when I finally slumped onto my stomach, a hot, searing pain located in my heart caused my entire body to tense … I was having a heart attack at the ripe old age of 20.

Much like the exaggerated self-doubt that had gotten me in this predicament in the first place, my self-diagnosis had proven to be hyperbolic. It turned out that, from the sheer number of energy drinks I had consumed in that short span, the inner lining of my heart had become badly inflamed, and that made it *feel* like a heart attack (pericarditis is what the doctor called it). I was treated immediately and put on strict bed rest.

During that painful time of recovery, I couldn't so much as watch a suspenseful movie scene without feeling a throbbing pain in my chest, so I simply refrained from any form of stimulus. I stopped drinking, smoking, socializing and self-caring—a true dopamine detox. Over the next few weeks, while I was performing an internal reset, I missed most of my final exams and was unable to plan, attend or celebrate my girlfriend's 21st birthday. I was ashamed, unwell and, once my head was clear, had ample time for self-reflection.

To this day, the regret I feel is not derived from scrambling to make money at the last minute, or the dangerous sales tactics I employed.

I learned the hard way that immediate gratification often leads to long-term failure.

Whether it was the pursuit of energy, a high, a thrill or lust, these were, in fact, not lifehacks. They were not shortcuts, they were short-lived. What's worse, the fake sources of energy and gratification that were keeping my body going were quite literally destroying my insides. What seemingly paid off the quickest came back to hurt me the most.

I eventually had the opportunity to present my girlfriend with a beautiful gold bracelet that I had saved up for. She liked it and put it on immediately, before getting teary-eyed in disappointment that I had missed her party. I consoled her and apologized.

"It's not your fault," she said, and she kissed me in gratitude.

My heart rate quickened; each throb brought a lingering jolt of pain to my chest.

Key Takeaway:	Lessons Learned:
Immediate gratification can lead to long-term failure.	- The pressure we put on ourselves can far outweigh the pressure from others. - Be wary of things (and people) that are all flash and no substance. - You only get one body; listen to it, take care of it.

Questions to ask yourself about your personal brand:

☐ Although this may be the quickest way, is it the *right* way?

☐ Am I prioritizing feeling good now over sustainable growth?

☐ When I can't afford monetary gestures, can I make up for it in time well spent?

Action Steps:

Thinking of trying a digital detox?

Here are the top five ways you can change your daily routine to limit the amount of time you are mindlessly scrolling through television, social media or any other activity you deem unhealthy.

#1. Read 10 pages of something that genuinely interests you.

#2. Journal (with a pen and paper) using the "free-flow method"—empty your thoughts onto the page, no stopping, no editing; simply let out the complexity of the emotions surrounding you at that moment. Set a timer and go.

#3. Find a new recipe, buy the ingredients and cook it.

#4. Go for a long walk, a bike ride or a swim.

#5. Ask yourself "what would a bored teenager from 1980 do?" When they didn't have phones, @ mentions or hundreds of channels, what did a bored teenager do to stimulate themselves?

Mirror at Macy's

"Vanity and pride are different things, though the words are often used synonymously. A person may be proud without being vain."
—Jane Austen

I would've been seven when it happened. I was in a department store, repetitiously making rounds between the racks of clothes that stood significantly taller than me, not-so-patiently waiting for my mother and sister to finish their shopping. I came to the end of an aisle in the shoe section and saw a mirror tilted toward me.

I had never seen a mirror angled this way, so I changed up my posture and facial expressions, slowly rolling my face back and forth and taking in the details of my features in perfect illumination.

I didn't look how I thought I looked. I surveyed myself deeply and intently.

"Oh, ho, ho!"

Around the end of the aisle, my father appeared; he'd been watching me from afar, the scoff practically falling out of his mouth as he approached.

"Checking yourself out? Don't be so vain."

I can't say if it's true for those of you who've grown up in the era that normalized the intimate relationship we have with the selfie (#unfiltered), but in the age directly preceding it, my father's dig had a lasting effect on me.

I didn't check up on myself for years after he made that comment; I didn't want to be vain.

It would appear others shared this same "lesson" when they were younger, and it has been (perhaps not so embarrassingly) engrained in them as it was in me. And so today, I have the pleasure of unteaching it, which I do in the form of a rather unassuming question:

"How often do you google yourself?"

Humans by nature become extremely uncomfortable at prolonged silence. It somewhat ironically sounds unnatural to them. And prolonged silence after I pose this question is exactly what I must sustain for seconds so painful that they feel like minutes, until someone breaks the quiet with a reluctant answer.

But why does it take so long? Because no one is jumping out of their chair to out themselves as the little boy staring at himself in the department store mirror—to do so would be vain.

When the answer finally comes, there are two confessions that most commonly follow. In fact, they're so common that they make up 99% of the responses I get:

1. I googled myself in error (e.g., I meant to type it into some other site).

2.   I did it but only as a shortcut—it's the quickest way
to get to my Facebook (it's not).

At this point, I ask the entire room to google themselves,
consciously and immediately. It's quite the sight to see—an
entire room full of heads dropping down in unison like
falling necks of flamingos gracefully plunging into the
water. But what re-emerges is nowhere near as
picturesque—quite the opposite, actually. The faces that
prop back up after those few precious seconds are
downright distraught. Why?

Because once they searched, they didn't like what they
found.

It's a painful lesson in personal branding; those who
don't regularly search for themselves do not know what
they'll discover. Anyone who regards it vain owns no
conversation, even when the topic being discussed is
themselves. They merely flow into it with as much prudence
as the blindfolded aiming at the dartboard, eyes closed,
fingers crossed and hoping for the bullseye. And all of this
is made worse by knowing that, today, most first
impressions are forged on Google. Search queries are the
new handshake. It's not enough to contribute to the results:
we need to own them—what shows up and (as importantly)
what doesn't.

So to seven-year-old me and for whomever else needs to
hear this: it's not vain to look at yourself, not digitally nor
physically. Looking at yourself deliberately is the first step
toward establishing the presence that you want to build, one
you are proud to project, no matter who else is watching. And
trust me, if you do this consciously, they'll be watching.

***

Personal Brand Activity:

GOOGLE YOURSELF

It's not vain, it's strategic.

In fact, it can also help heighten your own security and safety. Googling yourself is the first step to controlling the online conversation about you.

STEP 1: Type your full name within quotations marks (e.g., "Adam Rodricks") into the search bar of Google (or your search engine of choice). If you have a very common name, you may want to add another keyword qualifier such as your location or employer.

STEP 2: Scroll through the results to see which of these results have to do with you, as opposed to someone with the same name.

STEP 3: Evaluate whether the information available about you is advantageous to have shared or could be to your detriment, e.g., did you intend to have your Facebook profile set to public? Did you want your email address so readily available?

STEP 4: Take note of which results are showing up at the very top as these will likely be used by people who need to make a decision about you, whether that person is a friend, a potential employer or a date.

So why does this even matter?

- 8% of Internet users say they've asked someone to remove information about them that was posted online.[1]
- 4% of Internet users say they've had a bad experience because of embarrassing or inaccurate information online.[2]

Remember, every single thing that you do online has the potential to contribute to your online reputation. What does your search say about you?

Key Takeaway:	Lessons Learned:
It's not vain to look at yourself.	- Unlearning lessons is sometimes as important as learning new ones. - Monitoring and tracking your personal brand does not make you vain, it makes you strategic. - If you don't consciously search, you may not find the answer.

---

[1] Statistics Credit: https://www.backgroundchecks.org/blog/.
[2] Sources: Social Media for Learning: https://socialmediaforlearning.com/.

Questions to ask yourself about your personal brand:

☐ Have I assessed where my brand is today in terms of search rank, number of impressions and levels of engagement, to understand if the methods I employ are actually leading to progress?

☐ Are there search results of my brand I need to suppress as I work to accentuate others?

☐ In the absence of knowing where to go next, where can I look for an example of what to focus on?

Action Steps:

Season Pass

"Worrying does not take away tomorrow's troubles; it takes away today's peace."
—Randy Armstrong

Erma Bombeck once said that worrying is like a rocking chair: "It gives you something to do, but it doesn't get you anywhere." This is the story of the year I spent with my butt superglued to a rocking chair.

SPRING 2020

The nightly news continually flashed with headlines of COVID-19, but we assured our friends and family that it would not impact our plans to have a destination wedding. We took every news story headline with a grain of salt, disinterested and unbothered.

"Don't worry," I said to one guest who called, nervous after seeing the news of rising cases. "We're going to Cabo, come hell or high water. They can't stop us."

Six days later, the borders were closed, and our wedding was cancelled.

Devastated, we joined the long list of people who were forced to put their lives on hold. After a few weeks without any signs of hope, I knew I needed help.

I started reaching out to those close to me for advice on what to do. The first person who came to mind was Brian.

Brian had been my mentor since I was in my early twenties. He had short white hair and chunky blue glasses that looked far more fashion-forward than he truly was. Brian loved tweed, weed and wine, and he spoke in parables so poignant you could publish most conversations straight to Twitter. He was a master of insight and brevity. Most importantly, although Brian was constantly plagued by one illness or another, he was always in chipper spirits. It was his optimism I needed most now.

We agreed to meet once the lockdown had lifted.

SUMMER 2020

I sat in the coffee shop at the foot of his office building, blankly staring out the window while I waited. To the naked eye, there was no imminent threat. Children were laughing and chasing each other. There was no visible force that was supposedly tearing the world apart; it all seemed so normal. What was happening felt disproportionally unfair to us.

The thoughts swirled around like my coffee as I stirred, adding to the look of exasperation Brian undoubtedly noticed on my face when he walked in.

"Why me?" I asked unrhetorically as he sat down. "Everyone since the history of time ... hell, even during wartime! They've all been able to celebrate a wedding, but our damn luck this would happen now…!"

Over the course of the next hour, I spoke, and Brian listened. He offered little in terms of advice, and I thought maybe this was a mentoring exercise; he was waiting for me to arrive at the solution myself.

If this was indeed his plan, I failed harder than Snoop Dogg taking a drug test. On and on I went, hurling profanities and condemnations for the government's ineptitude and the airline's cowardice. My wrath left no one untouched, no matter how little actually fell within their control.

"She's bought her dress and I my tux," I continued. "What if they don't fit by the time we—"

"Adam—"

"Then there's the issue of our friends who work in the trades. We wanted to just go anyway, but they'd have to quarantine and lose pay and—"

"Adam," he pressed.

I looked up to see complete composure on his face. I was instantly reminded of who in this relationship was the mentor and, frankly, the only adult at the table.

"This is a waste of time," he said.

I opened my mouth to retort but no words came out.

"Good and bad things will happen in life. You just have to keep on keeping on and not stress over what you can't control."

"But what do I do?! What's going to happen to our wedding?"

"Whatever is going to happen is going to happen whether you worry or not. Do you agree?"

I did not agree.

"OK, if we can't agree on whether this is worth worrying about, perhaps we can reframe *the way* you worry."

I didn't see how any of this was going to get me to Cabo, but I humoured him.

"I want you to ask yourself if the things you worry about are going to matter in a day—"

"Of COURSE it's going to matter in a day, Brian!" I shot back vehemently.

"If the answer is yes," he continued calmly, "then will this problem matter in a week? A month? A year? Call me and tell me."

"Alright."

I reluctantly obeyed like a child who had just been scolded in front of his friends. We parted ways soon after I gave the coldest and most insincere "Thanks" I could offer.

The next week I didn't call, so Brian texted me to ask if the wedding situation was still bothering me.

"Obviously," I responded.

"OK," he said. "Text me again next week and let me know if anything changes."

This impersonal exchange continued for weeks until my fiancée and I made the hard decision to postpone the wedding indefinitely. I didn't even bother to tell Brian.

FALL 2020

Amidst all the doom and gloom as the pandemic waged on, my wife and I took a brisk autumn walk, and she played with my wedding band through our locked fingers.

"I still can't believe we're married," she smiled.

"I know. I was holding off posting anything in hopes we'd eventually have the big celebration, but since that isn't looking good, maybe it's time."

We walked home, and with my busy brain amassing captions about togetherness and love, I suddenly thought of Brian. Three months later, and he was right. We had our humble church ceremony, and we were married. I wasn't worried anymore.

I took out my phone and sent him a quick message:

"Hey Brian, long time! We didn't get to have that wedding, but we did get married, and you were right—it wasn't worth worrying about. How've you been?"

WINTER 2020

Winter brought with it the worst lockdown yet, and the extreme isolation was heightened by the fact that I still hadn't heard back from Brian.

With pictures of our humble ceremony now posted, I presumed he was annoyed that I didn't follow through on our mentorship as I had promised. I apologized in an email, then tried contacting him by phone but continually only got his voicemail.

Then one day, I saw the little "Online" button next to his name and I tried again.

"Hi, Adam."

I started to type out my apology as the next bit of text came in.

"This is Brian's wife. I'm just on here gathering some pictures for his funeral when I saw your message."

I read it several times ... sure I had misunderstood. In shock, I googled him and found the obituary.

SPRING 2021

I spent months processing Brian's death and re-reading every bit of correspondence we had had over the course of almost a decade.

Frequently, to help me cope, I came back to his comments on how to reframe worry; neither he nor I knew how important they'd be to put things into perspective.

Brian's questions should have shown me that as long as I eventually got to marry my wife, there was no need to worry. In my time of self-wallowing, I had failed to keep my eye on the prize (and my wife is indeed a prize I had no business "winning").

My late mentor's bittersweet lesson showed me that situations are often not changed by any amount of worrying, so we should never let our worries about tomorrow rob today of its joy.

While many of life's problems do indeed pass, other losses suffered are permanent, so we had best appreciate what little time we have together.

I hope the next time you feel the way I did, Brian's questions can help you to reframe what's truly worth worrying about. May it allow you to draw renewed perspective and strength for those you love, so we can be there for them while we still have the chance.

Thank you, Brian.

Key Takeaway:	Lessons Learned:
Reframe the way you worry: Will it matter in a year?	- Responding in anger will not turn out well; take a break to cool off first. - Time is our most precious resource, because unlike money, we don't know exactly how much of it we have left.

Questions to ask yourself about your personal brand:

☐ Although I'm upset now, will this impact me in a week? A month? A year?

☐ Have I been there for those I love? If not, can I take five minutes to do so now?

☐ Love can be expressed in many ways; can I show it in ways (in gestures, deeds, or writing) that can convey my feelings when I cannot express it personally?

Action Steps:

Are you worried about something? Try this three-step process to do something about it.

Step 1: Write down everything you're worried about in a list.

Step 2: Cross out all the factors that you've listed that you can't control.

Step 3: Make a plan to address all the factors that you can control.

Duplicity

"Whoever said 'never meet your heroes'
obviously had the wrong heroes." —Anonymous

I've made a lot of mistakes in my life and perhaps one of the biggest was idolizing a movie star. If you grew up with posters of Hollywood actors plastered on your bedroom walls, you might say infatuation was inevitable. And if you watched many of the movies that they starred in, you likely developed a deep fondness like I did. It was subconscious yet strong, and then I got to meet him.

I'm not going to mention names, and it truly doesn't matter who he is. For the purpose of this story, you can picture any A-lister whose face covers buildings, bus shelters or billboards. We are talking about a household name.

And that household name just happened to be in my city to promote his new product launch. He was launching exclusively at one of my company's stores, and I jumped at the chance to interview a man I so deeply admired.

The idea was simple: rather than doing static ads or written product reviews, we'd put my obsession on display, sitting me next to my Hollywood idol to do a one-on-one interview on camera, subtly promoting his product throughout.

I prepared tirelessly for this interview using a technique I call "conversational tennis." The best interviews I've ever conducted have been like a game of tennis. The dialogue keeps moving back and forth, much like the tennis ball in a rally over the net. I studied his nuances—particularly when he seemed to like or dislike something—to have non-verbal cues that I could adapt to on the fly as needed. I devoured every bit of his public life that had been released to his fans. I was ready for anything he could throw at me … except what he threw at me.

On the day of the interview, I arrived at a trendy, downtown advertising boutique. Think of any store you've wandered into and immediately felt was not "for you." I suppose to some it was approachable and understated, with brick wall backdrops and the noticeably neglected houseplants that littered the room like rows of groupies waiting off stage.

I greeted the crew and excitedly took my spot in one of the two bright-red chairs.

I shot looks over to the door every 10 seconds in between mental rehearsals of my introduction. *Firm handshake is critical*, I thought to myself.

Then he entered.

As grand as ever, he was flanked on either side like an army general. Totally unassuming to look at, but there was no mistaking his signature swagger and piercing blue eyes. *Just like in the movies*, I thought.

He huddled with his entourage of 10 or so in the corner while his publicist came forward and happily shook our hands.

Think of a time you were at a party and your crush walked in. As hard as you may have tried to focus on the conversation you were having, you just couldn't help but look over—where was she, what was she doing, had she noticed you? Distracted, I caught precisely none of the publicist's instructions; she could've been telling me to conduct the interview in Swahili and I would've nodded in agreement.

The lights dimmed and he finally came forward. He walked up to the red chairs and surveyed them both, peering right through me. I gestured him closer with a boisterous and warm greeting.

"I just want to say, it is an absolute honour to meet you."

The crew scuttled forward and outfitted him with his microphone in a fraction of the time they took to get me set up, which made sense given how precious his time was. He haphazardly lifted the back of his shirt as they pulled the wires through, and while he leaned forward to give them access, I attempted again to let him know just how lucky I knew I was.

"I've been watching you since I was a kid. I know everything there is to know about you and your new product."

"Great," he said flatly, his eyes now down as he tucked his shirt back in.

The crew dispersed and the heat of the lights let me know that they were now trained on each of us.

He finally looked up at me. I smiled in response, but he continued to stare blankly. The only way I could describe it: indifferent. His lack of energy or any type of warmth stirred an unevenness from within; surely, he knew we were all here for *him*, to make his product launch a success.

I tried once more. "We're going to have some fun today; I think I've got some questions that you may never have heard before."

Not a word of acknowledgement. I looked down at my notes to hide the disappointment that was now surely falling on my face.

"We're rolling," I could hear someone say. And before I could snap out of it, this A-lister who had given me precisely zero effort in the minutes before, slapped me on my knee and I looked up to see him chuckling as if I'd just delivered the punchline of a joke.

My jaw may have fallen open, but I refocused, slightly bewildered like a comedian hearing laughter to a setup line.

I knew it, I thought. *He just needed to warm up.* I sprung into action and returned the jovial energy he had mustered out of nowhere.

We spoke for 15 minutes, like best buds. I *felt* the rapport, the instant chemistry between us, and we didn't stumble in our discussion even once. He didn't miss a cue nor a setup line, even though we had never met, and we had never rehearsed. A born natural!

Someone yelled "Cut," and I almost exploded out of my chair. "That was AWESOME!" I exclaimed.

I was positively beaming ear to ear. Gratitude poured out of my mouth in bits of incoherent babble.

"That was such a cool experience, thank you so much for agreeing to do this. If you wouldn't mind before you leave, could I get you to sign our script for me, please?"

"What?" he shot back with palpable discontent.

We weren't buddies anymore.

Like a deer in the headlights, I said nothing. The fun-loving demeanour from just seconds before had completely disappeared, in its place nothing more than tangible irritation. I held out my notes, somewhat unsure.

"I brought my script, I was hoping you—"

He raised his palm to stop me.

"Nah, I don't want to do that," and he began to rip the wires from under his shirt.

I felt as though someone had just punched me in the stomach. I looked off toward the side of the room where everyone was still watching, feeling extremely embarrassed. I made eye contact with someone from my company who motioned for me to just let it slide, and my throat began to close ever so slightly. I swallowed hard and readied myself to face him again as if I was unphased and got refused requests like this all the time.

When I turned back to let him know it wasn't a big deal, he had already started toward the door.

In that moment, I didn't feel bad that I couldn't get an autograph.

I was disgusted that I wasn't even going to receive a "Thank you."

I made it a point to walk around that room and shake the hand of every single person who remained on set and helped us that day.

***

In the months that passed, friends asked me many times how the interview went and whether I liked the product. But most of all, people asked me how *he* was. I've never lied.

They say you should never meet your heroes because we create impossible expectations for them to live up to, but that day a role model I held in high regard didn't even live up to my standard of everyday decency.

Be kind and be genuine. The cost of insincerity is far too great, and the way you make people feel will speak volumes in rooms where you aren't even present.

***

Social Engagement Activity:

HOW TO PLAY CONVERSATIONAL TENNIS

Whether you're looking to liven up a presentation or just make the most out of an opportunity with someone, try a technique called "playing conversational tennis."

The idea is that great conversations resemble a game of tennis: they feature back-and-forth rallies where two people are heavily involved, as things build in both pace and enjoyment.

Sometimes these "rallies" will go on for hours; other times they'll provide you with a short but important opportunity to make a lasting impression on someone through a fulfilling interaction.

So how exactly do we play conversational tennis?

These are the three keys to playing conversational tennis effectively:

TIP #1: Much like in an actual game of tennis, focusing on your opponent is key.

Let's face it, people love talking about themselves.

But if you were to try this by simply sustaining a conversation by making it all about you, the other person is going to feel left out, bored or ignored. Instead use this focus on the other person's feelings, thoughts or experiences when you genuinely wish to know more about what they're saying.

TIP #2: Don't just hit it back, take the time to rally with the other person.

You may think the goal of conversational tennis is to be quick moving. That's not the case. Instead of just throwing a barrage of questions or comments at your subject, mix it up by asking a follow-up question, or adding to the conversation with your own thoughts and experiences.

TIP #3: Body language.

Much like an opponent who has been beaten mentally and is simply waiting for the formality of the game's final whistle, you can tell how engaged someone is in conversation from across the room.

Sharing open body language (eyebrow raise, mirroring motions, gazing, smiling) is an invitation for more in the same way that closed body language (hands in pocket, crossing your arms, fidgeting) can represent a lack of engagement. Project open body language as much as possible during conversational tennis.

The key to good conversations, much like a good game of tennis, is to keep the ball moving, skillfully play what you're given and build a rapport much like you would a rally.

Sources:

http://simplypsyched.com/conversational-tennis/
https://www.scienceofpeople.com/body-language-examples/

Key Takeaway:	Lessons Learned:
Being fake is costly.	- Choose your role models wisely. - The best exchanges feature "conversational tennis": the back-and-forth flow keeps it engaging. - Regardless of social standing, showing decency to others is a true sign of class.

Questions to ask yourself about your personal brand:

- ☐ What do I admire about this person? Am I aware of their less desirable traits too?
- ☐ Would including an element of audience interaction make my presentation more engaging?
- ☐ How can I show my appreciation to others using my words and/or actions?

Action Steps:

Confessions from My Commute

*"There is no such thing as an attention span.
There is only the quality of what you are
viewing."* —Jerry Seinfeld

In the summer of 2006, I got my first part-time job, which made it necessary for me to take the train into the city. It was all very official. There were paycheques and everything. I wasn't quite ready for it as evidenced by my showing up to the office on the hottest day of the year in shorts. I wasn't a very bright young man, but what I lacked in intelligence I more than made up in regulated body temperature.

Knowing I needed to fit in better with my fellow nine to fivers, I would peep curiously at what they would do on the train ride every morning, hoping for more insight into normal adult behaviour. I distinctly remember the patterns of the three other people who invariably shared my row of seats every day, because I studied them to avoid another shorts-like catastrophe.

There was Mom of the Year, a mother who called home the second we had boarded to provide her husband with the most descriptive instructions on how he was going to somehow manage to keep the kids alive until she returned home that evening. Next to her and directly across from me was Mr. Jenga. Mr. Jenga was a tall man in a beige overcoat who had the most fascinating sleep patterns: every so often he'd nod off into a deep sleep until his body began swaying with the motion of the train and inevitably dipped so low that he got the sensation of falling. He would abruptly wake up in a tizzy, often sprawling out violently to brace himself from a fall (I'm aware that this description is much more reminiscent of Slinky than Jenga, but I was 17 and I wore shorts to the office—clearly intelligence wasn't my forte). Finally, next to him was a young woman who taught me a lesson I carry to this day.

You see, I never once caught her name as she never took a call like Mom of the Year, and she never looked at me—not even momentarily in horror as she was jolted awake like Monsieur Jenga. So we'll just call her Elon Musk ... sorry, Elona Musk. From the moment Elona boarded to the moment we arrived at Union Station, her eyes were glued to her phone screen. She was a master of multitasking. Once I realized her gaze was unbreakable, I would just blatantly stare, incredulous at how fast her eyes would move and her finger ... her fingers darted so quickly that I'm fairly certain they never completely left the screen. She had this ability to absorb information at an alarming rate and she never really took breaks either. Invariably she was the most interesting of our quartet and the subject of most of my stalking ... research. Once I saw her pause momentarily to yawn, and I got so excited I held out a Kleenex. She still didn't flinch. And every day, Elona would switch from app to app, texting now and then, but furiously scrolling through her feeds as if it was some sick game: *Finish by the time we arrive or a loved one will die.*

So what did a smartphone–obsessed commuter teach me that I'm sharing with you? Just what we're up against.

When I write content, I write for Elona. Because I imagine that with any piece of content—no matter how well-written it is, or how eye-catching a visual is attached—my opportunity to make an impact can be gone in the flash of an eye, especially if she is on the other end. So whenever I think of mailing it in, or publishing content for content's sake, I hear the train pulling into the station in my mind, and I imagine producing something of a high enough quality that maybe it'll find its way onto her feed long enough for her finger to leave the screen.

✴ ✴ ✴

Social Media Activity:

HOW TO WRITE A GREAT SOCIAL MEDIA POST

I'm sorry.

If you googled "how to go viral" and landed here, I can't help you. I can, however, give you a formula that will help maximize your chances of generating quality engagement on your social media posts.

The anatomy of a great post is:

STEP 1: Add something of value with everything you share.

+

STEP 2: Include a click-through direction, e.g., "Register now," "Click here to learn more."

+

STEP 3: Attach an eye-catching visual from a site like https://www.pexels.com/ or https://unsplash.com/ (free from copyright) to disrupt feeds and stop people from scrolling past your content.

=

Quality post.

EXAMPLE

I put this exact formula to work on my own social media content and regularly enjoy reach and engagement that spreads far beyond my own network of followers.

As an example, in the first week of January 2022, I came across a listicle entitled "22 Ways to Supercharge Productivity in 2022." I thought:

Great! I need this.

But the article was full of rubbish.

At this point, I had a choice. I could "flame" the author for wasting my time, I could carry on my way silently or I could implement the formula above.

So instead, I commented on the article:

Interesting take. I was surprised not to see my favourite productivity app listed so I'll share it here. It's called Evernote, and it enables me to track my notes regardless of the platform

I'm on. For those interested, here is a link to download it free from the app store: https://apps.apple.com/us/app/evernote-notes-organizer/id281796108.

And I kid you not, by simply adding value, telling people where to click and having the rich media snippet populate in my comment to break up the otherwise dense wall of text, I generated more engagement on my comment than the article itself had.

The best part? I didn't need a PhD or hours of research to make an impactful post. I simply drew authentically from my own experiences and followed a formula.

And you can too.

Key Takeaway:	Lessons Learned:
Attention spans are short; make it count.	- Our opportunities to make an impact are shorter than ever, meaning our content needs to be of a higher quality than ever. - A greater understanding of our target audience is critical to the success of our content strategy. - Make sure your brand and your content answer the "so what?" question at every step.

Questions to ask yourself about your personal brand:

☐ Why would I care? Why would I share?

☐ What can I do to disrupt my audience's feed?
(e.g., include an engaging visual, ask a question,
present a poignant statistic, etc.)

☐ What pain-point or value proposition am I
addressing for my target audience?

Action Steps:

The Death of the Instagram Model

*"You don't have to be a 'person of influence' to
be influential. In fact, the most influential
people in my life are probably not even aware of
the things they've taught me."*
—Scott Adams

How much do you trust?

I usually have that split-second hesitation before I give
my car keys to a valet. *What if* creeps into my mind. I used to
think I was alone, but the way that we give (or lack) trust is
fascinating to examine.

Have you heard the story of Arianna Renee? Arianna, or
@Arii on Instagram, is a Miami-based social media
influencer. She catapulted to online stardom in 2019 and had
more than 2.6 million followers, all before she could legally
buy alcohol.

Of course, with her account blowing up, Arianna wanted
to monetize on her platform by starting her own clothing
line. The company producing her fashion brand informed

her that for her to go into production, her first run of
products needed to sell a modest 36 shirts.

And she couldn't do it.

Now you're probably thinking, selling 36 of something
doesn't seem like that much, especially if you have a Girl
Guide in the family. But when this story hit the
Twittersphere, every marketer worth a damn turned to their
colleague and asked the same question: What is the value of
2.6 million followers if you can't sell 36 shirts to your
audience?

You could probably point to a poor marketing plan
leading up to the launch or an aesthetic that didn't match the
brand Arianna had built on the platform as major
contributors to this failure. But here's another thought: What
if the influencer bubble is bursting because we don't trust
them?

It's been known for a long time that celebrities can be
hired to promote products and doing so often does give
brands boosted reach, access to an untapped audience and
often a spike in sales results. That's why they do it. But as
these partnerships come to an end, the influencers and their
followings move on to the next one, leaving brands they've
worked with in largely the same position they started. So was
there any long-term benefit of this partnership? Was there a
better way to build relationships to sustain growth and
engagement online than essentially paying for it every time
you needed to sell something?

Enter the micro-influencer.

You may have heard the term; a micro-influencer (or
nano-influencer) is a highly influential person, but on a much
smaller scale. Often, their niche is hyper-specific, and

although this usually means they have a significantly smaller following than most celebrities you've seen plastered on ads, micro-influencers are known for having intensely engaged audiences.

In other words, when micro-influencers talk, their networks trust, and they listen.

What's more, micro-influencing isn't some passing trend that only affects sales on Instagram; it's at play in our own lives every single day.

If you think about the last time you made a big purchase like a television or a car, you probably didn't make that decision in isolation (unless you're a tech aficionado or a gearhead). Odds are, on a purchase that mattered a great deal given how much money you were spending, you asked for the opinion of one or a few trusted sources you knew. And that's not even to say that you knew them personally. Consumers make decisions every day based on testimonials from complete strangers. The demand for anonymous testimonials is so high that entire farms of fake reviewers started cropping up—picture a whole factory full of people whose only job all day is to continually click "five stars" on Amazon. Once again, we take one step toward establishing trust, and two steps backward to destroying it.

But unlike celebrities who may or may not command the spotlight by the time next year's product launches are upon us, personal relationships usually persist and grow.

I have a friend named Brandon. He's a political junkie but you'd never know it. He doesn't talk about political campaigns, nor does he shove his viewpoints down anyone's throats. That's partially what attracted me to Brandon when I needed a trusted opinion on who to vote for.

To be clear, when I talked to Brandon, I never asked him, "Who do I vote for?" Instead, he'd offer the best places I could go for unbiased opinions on party platforms so I could make my own decision. Watching the nightly news gave me anxiety, and frankly, the campaign trail evolved so quickly it made my head spin. All I needed was a trusted source to give me a trusted source so I could make my own decision. And Brandon provided me a list.

It worked so well that I did it again for the next election. And the next election. And soon I was telling my other friends, many who were contemplating not voting at all, to do the same. Before he knew it, Brandon had built up a small network of impressionable voters, for whom he could share sources to educate themselves. It scaled so much, he now puts his lists of resources in a nonpartisan newsletter because it's just more efficient. Brandon has become a micro-influencer on the backs of people like me: those who consider voting to be our civic duty, but don't particularly enjoy politics and are exhausted by keeping up with traditional media. And he did it all through a network of referrals predicated on trust.

But perhaps you aren't politically inclined, and you don't buy products on social media. Is micro-influencing still relevant to you?

Think about something virtually every adult in the Western world does: shopping.

If you walked into an electronics store 20 years ago, you would have noticed a stark difference from today; the number of employees in their blue shirts walking around the store, most with lineups of customers waiting to talk to them. Before the internet fit into the palms of our hands and we needed the advice of an expert to make a big purchasing decision, store associates were often it (despite the obvious conflict of interest that their commission could bring into the equation).

Fast forward to today, if you walk into those same stores, you'll notice a distinctly different consumer behaviour: the customer walks in and often heads directly to the department or item they need. And when they arrive in front of the item they're thinking of buying, instead of looking around for someone to help them, they look down and bury their head in their phone. Why? That's where the experts and our trust reside now.

The Instagram influencer business model has died. Or at the very least, it's changed. We don't need to tap into large, established voices because any voice now has the potential to be amplified. The best part of social media is that it gave everybody a microphone! (Coincidentally, the worst part of social media is that it gave *everybody* a microphone.)

Although technology has increased our ability to trust others, we don't trust the technology itself; in fact, far from it. But when we need help to make our decisions, technology has awarded us a way in which we can trust in each other. And if we can't rely on each other, we've got much bigger problems. Trust me!

***

The Influencer Partnership Activity:

HOW TO WRITE A PERSUASIVE PITCH LETTER

Over the years, I've read hundreds of pitch letters from influencers and bloggers hoping to collaborate with big brands.

While the vast majority of them sucked something fierce, there were those select few that not only stood out, but were also accepted and became partners.

Of these influencer partnerships, the pitch letters all had the same three elements that made them successful. Let's look at how you can write a persuasive pitch for blogger and influencer relations.

1. **Introduce yourself, how you came across their product/service and why you like it** – Too many people start pitch letters without the very basics of an introduction. We cannot overlook the fact that the vast majority of pitch letters serve as the first formal point of introduction between the influencer and the brand. Start at the beginning and be specific about why you like the brand.

2. **Sell yourself** – The whole purpose of you reaching out is not to ask the brand for a favour; you have something to offer them too! Show them what you can do by sharing some statistics about your audience, reach or recent accolades that answer the question, "Why would YOU want to work with ME?"

3. **Leave the door open for next steps** – You've made your case, now point them in your direction should a collaboration be of interest. Leave them with your contact information, handles, website—however you wish to continue the conversation.

EXAMPLE – THE INFLUENCER PITCH EMAIL

Dear John,

My name is Adam Rodricks and I'm the influencer behind www.adamrodricks.com and @adamrodricks.

I've been a long-time fan of **ABCBrand** *and I recently saw an ad for* **TheProduct***; after doing some research, I realized this was definitely something I would buy because* **BiggestBenefitGoesHere***.*

Recently, I passed **[# of followers]** *and* **[# of page views or subscribers]** *so I wanted to reach out and discuss a possible partnership. In exchange for* **[your ask]***, I would love to write a 500-word post about* **TheProduct***, complete with custom photography; I'd be happy to promote it extensively across my channels as well. I think* **TheProduct** *would be of serious interest to my audience, and I'd love the opportunity to share it on* **[your main platform(s)]***.*

If possible, I'd love to include a quote from a company spokesperson to give my post an extra-personal touch.

I'd be more than happy to send you my press kit or rate card for further discussion if this is of interest.

If you'd like more information about me you can check out my **[blog URL]***,* **[@social handle]** *or* **[vlog/podcast]***.*

Thanks so much for your time,

Adam

Key Takeaway:	Lessons Learned:
Establishing trust is key.	- The way we trust brands has changed, but we still trust each other. - You don't have to be famous to have meaningful influence. - Reviews, endorsements and testimonials are an effective and powerful way to rapidly grow trust.

Questions to ask yourself about your personal brand:

- ☐ What is the value of my brand? Can it compel my audience to take action?
- ☐ Have I cultivated the expertise in my craft to make me a trusted source?
- ☐ Can I grow relationships with partners, other brands and audience members to introduce my brand into conversations I am currently not a part of?

Action Steps:

The Key to Power

"A referral is the key to the door of resistance."
—Robert Foster Bennett

Have you ever approached a vacant restaurant or food vendor only to see a line materialize behind you immediately?

Humans crave validation and one form this often comes in is referrals. Nobody wants to be the first one to try the new Indian restaurant on the corner, but if they see four people waiting patiently in the cold, there's no other conclusion to arrive at: it must be good.

I found myself in one such line when my heart was most full. I had just moved downtown and began dating my (now) wife around the same time. Things progressed quickly and, before long, I had made up my mind that I wanted to give her a key to my apartment. It was a big move; I'm a private person and before this, I'd have said the largest thing I'd shared with a significant other was a plate of dessert.

Nevertheless, I felt ready, and I was in the mood for a grand gesture.

I had noticed this custom key cutter in the underground concourse on my walks home from work and, because the lines were always long, thought this would be the perfect place to make my gift. Clearly, this store's reputation was all I needed to know so I joined the end of the line, halfway out the door. After I queued up, I buried my face in my phone, every now and then peeking at the counter to the very animated key cutter and the customers he was serving.

I popped my headphones in and started playing "our song" while I thought about all of the different ways I could present the key. *I could put it in a box that was contained inside a bigger box and so on and so forth. I could stage some sort of fake "locked out" scenario, culminating in the gifting of the key to save the day, forever a story for us to tell.* As I lost myself in the possibilities, I stepped forward, and something started to drown out the music in my ears.

It was yelling.

I lowered my left earbud to get a better sense of the commotion.

"Is it a regular key?" the store owner demanded.

"Yes, yes," said the person in front of me, now front of the line. She was a short, portly woman draped in purple who from the back very much resembled a blueberry.

She dug deep in her coat pockets and shuffled to produce the key on the counter. It looked like mine.

"THIS?" the man exclaimed.

"This is not a regular key. This is an apartment key. Let me explain something to you."

And he banged a picture down on the counter showing all of the different types of keys.

His tone was condescending, and I noticed others were peering up to see what the hubbub was, hoping to avoid it themselves. *Should I have done more research to prepare for this?*

The store owner barked at the woman, explaining the different types of keys, slamming down on the picture he was describing. The keyman scolded her for not knowing the difference between her key and what she was asking for, before warning that this was not, in fact, a standard request—it would take longer and cost more.

"Well, how much more?" she asked politely but firmly.

"You think this is easy for me to do?"

At this point, I started to turn my own key over in my hand, wondering what I, too, was missing.

"It'll be at least an hour—and seventy dollars."

"Seventy dollars?!" she exclaimed. "That's absurd!"

"Are you calling me a cheat?" He was now booming over the counter, clearly ready to engage in a fight he had picked many times before. The short lady recoiled slightly, obviously not expecting this simple question to escalate as badly or as quickly as it had.

She stepped back in partial retreat, bumping into me and, unknowingly, tagging me into action.

"Excuse me," I said to her.

"My key is like your key, and I just saw on my phone it can be done just around the corner for—"

"Who the hell are you?" the man bellowed, his crosshairs now clearly set on someone trying to steal his business.

I tried to continue instructing her on the next-closest store, but he started around the corner, and I was suddenly very aware of the closing distance between us. I puffed my chest up and held my ground, while the blueberry retreated behind me and my outreached arm showing her my phone.

"You come into my store, and you take my customers?"

"I'm not t—"

And as he berated me, his spittle found its way onto my glasses. The remaining straggles of hair on his otherwise smooth and shiny head were now inches from mine and I, too, was getting hot under the collar, feeling the brunt of his anger for trying to diffuse the situation.

"Get out. Get OUT!" he shouted. And I pulled the right earbud out too.

"I'm going," I said, raising my hands to show I was leaving, but I knew I wasn't quite done.

"And I'll be sure to leave a Google review too."

Silence followed.

I half turned to see if he was quietly approaching, mid-lunge to attack or maybe reaching for something behind his counter I'd want no part of. Instead, I saw him standing shocked and still.

His entire demeanour had changed. It was as if Super Mario had collided with an enemy and become half his initial size.

"You'll what? You can't review me; you are not a customer!"

Very quickly, the battleground had shifted, and now I was the one in a position to explain the intricacies of my work to the unknowing.

"Watch me."

He didn't say another word. As the human blueberry and I turned to leave the store, we noticed the long line up behind us had completely dissipated and we were able to make haste without any obstructions in our way.

Still furious, the lady and I walked around the block to the big hardware store and submitted our keys to be copied, for a quarter of the price. As we were waiting, I typed up the Google review and showed it to her. Although she confirmed my recounting was accurate, she was unfamiliar with the platform and so she was hesitant to say much more. Evidently, while I was still fuming, she had let it go.

"I don't understand," she said. "We didn't actually buy anything. Why would anyone online believe us over him?"

Stories don't have to be personal to be powerful. Customers every day take the word of people they don't know in hopes that they can together learn from our collective experiences and avoid the follies of those who have gone the road before.

She thanked me for all my help, and we parted ways, but not before she waved and informed me excitedly that she would tell her kids to "review my Google."

I thought about clarifying for her, but something told me she had been corrected enough for one day.

Key Takeaway:	Lessons Learned:
Testimonials are powerful, even when second-hand.	- An experience doesn't have to be personal to be powerful. - Humans crave validation when it comes to the brands we trust. - A good experience can often make up for a brand's other shortcomings (e.g., years of experience, price, etc.).

Questions to ask yourself about your personal brand:

- ☐ What questions are being asked of my brand? Are the answers readily available to those seeking them?
- ☐ Who are my biggest advocates and how can I cultivate an audience around them?
- ☐ What hesitations would someone have about my brand? What can I do to address them upfront?

Action Steps:

Harness the power of positivity by leaving a customer review:

Gain exposure for your recommendations while also paying it forward using these six simple steps:

Step 1: Think of a recent and positive purchase experience that you've had.

Step 2: Choose a reputable review platform to submit your feedback. Some reputable review sites are:

Facebook	Amazon	Yelp	TripAdvisor
G2 (B2B)	Google My Business	Glassdoor	Angie's List

Step 3: Be specific in your review. Some prompts to help your customer testimonial stand out are: What about the interaction or purchase did you appreciate? How did they make you feel? Would you shop there again?

Step 4: Aim to write a review at least 3–4 sentences in length.

Step 5: After one week, revisit your review on the site and behold its reach! Better than some social posts we've authored, right?

Step 6: Look at other reviews on the same page; what factors do the most "helpful" or "liked" reviews have in common? Keep these in mind for your own brand's goals in the future.

Do the Owl Thing

*"I've learned that people will forget what you
said, people will forget what you did, but people
will never forget how you made them feel."*
—Maya Angelou

Tom Keiser is a visionary.

Since moving into leadership within the technology sector, he's spearheaded incredible growth in both revenue and talent acquisition at the companies he's helped, most recently as the CEO of Vancouver-based social media software giant Hootsuite. We met at Collision, one of the largest technology conferences in the world, where we were both speakers on the topic of social media.

I was struggling with writing this book, and I thought speaking to him would be the perfect opportunity to get some much-needed advice.

I readied myself with an armlong list of questions—hard-hitting stuff; I was going to make the most of our short time together. When he entered, I greeted him like an old friend from school and promptly decided that the entire list of questions I had prepared was far too intense to jump straight into.

"Basketball," I blurted out.

"I read online you think you have a nice jump shot," I continued. "Who, in your opinion, has the sweetest shooting form in the NBA?"

I saw Tom's brow furrowing for a second, and then his shoulders dropped. As a Bay Area native near San Francisco, his answer should have been obvious to me.

"Steph Curry has the nicest shot in the game."

The night before, Curry had scored 49 points and we made small talk about that. All the while, I looked down at my list of questions, still feeling too uncomfortable to dive into heavier topics like how the pandemic had shifted his leadership style, what it was like coaching people you've never met and infinitely more important questions about equality.

Now, I wasn't nervous about having this very necessary conversation; I was nervous because I didn't feel I had earned the trust to ask such intimate and personal questions. In business, so much of what we say is predicated on earning a seat at the table, and in this instance, I had not. At least not yet, so I decided to forego the script and speak from the heart.

"I want to thank you," I started.

"What for?" asked Tom, half-expecting me to say the interview had come to a close after some brief banter about basketball's greats.

And I began telling him this story.

"Ten years ago, the CEO of Staples Canada, Steve Matyas, took a chance on me. I approached him with the business case to start up the company's new social media accounts. I wanted to create a presence on Twitter to field customer queries, and I wanted to use Hootsuite to do it."

Tom leaned forward, intrigued about what this story might say about his company, and so I continued.

"I joined the CEO of Staples in his large and yet unintimidating boardroom for my pitch. I showed Steve the deck and then Steve, always warm, gently pressed me for my rationale. 'I want nothing more than to help our customers, Adam. But do you *know* what people do on Twitter?'"

Of course, he was right. At the time, Twitter was rapidly becoming the gutter of the internet; it was little more than vitriol—incoherent arguments and brand defamation in a public forum. Why would the company's CEO willingly sign up to expose our brand to this?

"'I know, I know,' I acknowledged.

"'But if our customers are at 10/10 levels of upset and on the verge of leaving us, I'd love to start by acknowledging their concerns head on, in hopes that we can bring their anger down to a level where it's possible to have the conversation about saving their business.'

"I saw it on Steve's face. The realization that I too was customer-centric. I left his office, and the next morning I got a voicemail from his staff that simply said, 'Tell Adam to do that owl thing, the hoot service.' And that was the start of my career in social media."

As I finished, Tom erupted in laughter. He reared his head back and repeated the final line.

"That reminds me of a similar story," said Tom.

I looked down at my list of questions like it was an old toothbrush, completely essential to me yesterday, and now useless, ready to be discarded.

"Back when I was at Zendesk, Niantic had just released the mobile app Pokémon GO."

The magnitude of this statement is lost on no one who owned a mobile device in the year 2016; Pokémon GO was a global phenomenon.

"They were a client and when we looked up their transaction numbers, we watched them skyrocket to the point they literally passed Uber in the number of users.

"And all this while we knew three things: we knew they were a small company, we knew they were ill-equipped to deal with this unprecedented growth, as evidenced by their lowest-level subscription to Zendesk, and we knew their office was across the street from ours in San Francisco.

"We walked over there that afternoon, and upon showing them how we could benefit their userbase, they jumped at our solution that helped scale their exploding business."

I snapped back to earth.

This was the point where Tom was looking for the "aha" moment to register on my face, but I hadn't come to any such epiphany, so he spelled it out for me.

"Sometimes, the best story you can tell is the one that benefits the customer."

So often we become fixated on ourselves, and we forget that for us to do better business we need to keep our audience top of mind. It may be your company, but you are *not* the hero of the story (at least not in your customers' eyes). In their lives they have problems, and we are the connectors to solutions.

That customer-centric focus helped launch my career, and I have leaders like Tom and Steve to thank. Little did I know the same philosophy also helped take one of the largest mobile apps in the history of the world to the next level.

To be successful in business, your customer doesn't need to know how much you know—they need to know how much you care.

***

Define Your Audience Activity:

HOW TO DETERMINE YOUR TARGET AUDIENCE

When a brand says, "Our ads are ineffective," do you know what I've found to be the most common problem?

Their ads are all about them.

I don't care whether you're running a single restaurant or a multinational corporation, having a solid understanding of your audience is critical to your success.

As such, every single piece of content you put out should keep THEM top of mind.

It may be difficult to think about your audience as a whole, but understanding your customers will make your brand far more capable of adapting to changes in your audience's needs and wants.

So what are the most important factors in understanding our audience? Here are the top 10 insights you should collect and analyze to better understand your target audience:

1. Age
2. Sex
3. Location

4. Occupation (or industry of work)
5. Hobbies
6. Household income
7. Social platform(s) of choice
8. Favourite brands
9. Values
10. Desires

Writing these down together helps to form an example target audience persona. With this in mind, it will help you to focus your content and branding efforts to your ideal target market.

Now you may be thinking, *Great. This would be very useful, but I have little to none of this information.*

If that's the case, consider these questions while you dive deeper into available research or your customer data:

- What is the problem in my audience's lives that I am solving?
- What is the value that I add to my audience?
- What would my audience say is the impact that I have on their lives?

Customers are the hero of their own stories, and we are merely the connectors to solutions. When you understand your answers to the questions above, you will be better able to speak to your audience even if you aren't quite sure who they are yet.

Key Takeaway:	Lessons Learned:
Always keep your audience top of mind.	- The best strategy is one that can adapt to a myriad of situations and challenges. - People need to be heard: Acknowledging dissatisfaction is often the first step to correcting it. - The hero of a brand's story is the customer, not you.

Questions to ask yourself about your personal brand:

- ☐ Is my brand story focused on my customer's solution?
- ☐ Do I know my audience's pain points, or have I made assumptions about what I think they need?
- ☐ Have I shown my audience how much I care about them, or am I simply talking about myself?

Action Steps:

Orchestrating Viral: What Do Silentó and Seth Rogen Have in Common?

> *"Virality isn't born, it's made."*
> —Jonah Berger, *Contagious*

Can you plan to go viral?

It's as offensive of a question as I've been asked, right up there with "What's she doing with you?" and "What's that smell?" accompanied with a telling glance in my general direction.

According to Urban Dictionary (which I confidently cite as the ultimate authority on internet definitions, as *Webster's* may be to everything else), to "go viral" is to share something that spreads rapidly through a population by being frequently shared with a number of individuals.

So by the very definition, YOU cannot plan to go viral. PEOPLE, as in plural, make things go viral.

Even though you can't plan for something to spread widely and successfully, marketers have never been shy about promising it in pitches. I can't tell you how many boardroom presentations have included "Step 2: Go Viral," to my noticeable chagrin. They're almost always wrong.

But if someone were able to orchestrate a way to go viral, how would they do it?

The answer is through rap music. At least that's the only way I've ever seen it achieved. Twice.

In my life, I've come across exactly two stories of people who intended to go viral, who then did go viral and who I actually believe had the tools to facilitate such a thing: rapper Silentó and actor Seth Rogen.

For those unfamiliar with the name Silentó, you certainly would know him as the artist behind the 2015 smash hit "Watch Me (Whip/Nae Nae)." It took the world by storm, generating over 80 million views on YouTube and peaking at number three on the US Billboard Hot 100.[3]

Going by the Chinese zodiac, 2015 was the year of the goat. Going by pop culture, it was the year of the Whip. The dance that the popular song was based on has been performed by people the world over, each similarly adding their own flare to the cultural phenomena that were the Twist, the Dougie and my personal favourite, the Macarena.

Everything seemed like a dream come true, a stroke of good luck for Silentó. Except for one thing: he didn't seem at all surprised by the overnight success of his debut single. In fact, he said it was planned.

Silentó recorded the smash hit when he was 17 years old in his basement and uploaded it to SoundCloud. I know what you're thinking: This doesn't seem like a "sure thing" for an unsigned kid to bank on; why was he so sure?

---

[3] https://djbooth.net/features/2016-02-danceon-silento-whip-nae-nae-dance-craze.

After his song had generated 100,000 streams on SoundCloud, Capitol Records approached him, signed him and produced an accompanying music video to release alongside the single. Here's where things got shady.

The Whip's sudden popularity was then put in the hands of DanceOn, a company whose business is quite literally to create viral dance hits. DanceOn then had their network of approximately 50 Vine, YouTube and Instagram influencers upload their own versions of the dance to the whopping tune of an additional 50 million views. And just like that, the seemingly organic dance challenge spread like fake wildfire, and the entire ordeal left me wanting a shower.

By contrast, Seth Rogen knew his next move would go viral at a time when he and James Franco were already A-list celebrities.

Whereas Silentó was an unproven artist and came across as delusional or arrogant when he said it was his plan to go viral all along, Rogen's surety in himself could be construed as confidence earned through a well-documented track record of success in the public eye.

In his memoir *Yearbook*, Rogen recalls working on the production of his upcoming movie *The Interview* when Kanye West dropped the music video for his song "Bound 2." If you've never seen it, I'll save you four minutes: It's utterly terrible, and that's coming from a Kanye West fan.

But its sheer cringiness led Rogen and co-star James Franco to think it was so easy to make fun of, it's not a matter of who should do it, but rather who would do it first. So they did! Shot-for-shot they impersonated Kanye West and Kim Kardashian on the back of a motorcycle, and all the while, Seth knew it would be gold:

"Making viral videos is impossible, in that you don't actually know what's gonna go viral. [...] The whole time we were making it, we were like 'There's zero percent chance it doesn't go everywhere instantly. It will go viral. And it very much did.'"[4]

***

So how do you plan to go viral? Easy! You either pay to manipulate your audience into thinking what they're seeing is genuine user-generated content, or you first become an A-list celebrity who then produces absurdly timely content because you were already in production on your super–big budget blockbuster film, and you personally know Kanye. So you're confident there will be minimal backlash and even if there is, who cares because you're super rich and can pay to defend yourself in court, and I think you get my point.

You cannot plan to go viral. Plan instead to create something of value. Ask yourself two questions before you even think of hitting "Enter," regardless of what platform you're on. And I promise this will work out far better for you than any viral plan you may concoct. Your two most important questions:

Why would I care? And... Why would I share?

---

[4] (Seth Rogen, *Yearbook*, Page 171).

Key Takeaway:	Lessons Learned:
Don't plan to go viral, plan to create value.	- Don't believe everything you read: Clout can be manufactured. - Social media is absolutely a "pay to play" environment. - Be vigilant with your content consumption: The objective of most campaigns is to look effortless and organic.

Questions to ask yourself about your personal brand:

- ☐ What is the value that my brand is bringing to my audience?
- ☐ Have I thought critically about the authenticity of the content I'm seeing?
- ☐ Does my plan rely on going viral? (If so: time for a new plan.)

Action Steps:

Want to move the needle on social, but strapped for time?

Try this 15-minute structure when you next log on to maximize your efficiency on social:

Minutes 1–5: Author a piece of content. If you're not sure what to say, share an existing piece of content and simply add an insight, a fresh perspective, or a thoughtful question.

Minutes 6–10: Engage with your existing network. Go through your feed with the aim of commenting, "liking" and even resharing what resonates with you.

Minutes 11–15: Grow your network by discovering new people to follow. Make use of the "People You May Know" suggestions and connect thoughtfully with customized invites when possible (e.g., on LinkedIn).

Trigger Fingers: Part I

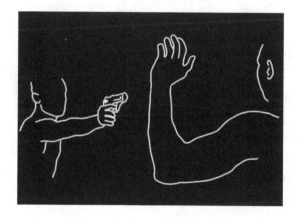

I never thought it would go like this:

My gun is pointed, and this next decision could be the last of my life.

What was going through my head to get to this place, now I can't even remember.

I squeeze slowly.

I'm bracing for the bang.

Will it be jarring like in the movies?

I instinctively raise my weapon to show I mean business.

***

The single most common question I get asked to weigh in on: "Is social media bad for us?" And my answer: "It's like a gun."

Most people take this as a negative affirmation but that's not at all what I mean.

Yes, social media, much like a gun, is used to cause harm to others and ourselves.

But can a tool itself, whatever its design, be inherently bad or does it take human intervention to become evil? Have you ever heard of an evil hammer, which was hellbent on nothing but stubbing fingers and bending nails? Probably not. If I told you those two things happened to me, and I pointed my (stubbed) finger at the hammer, you'd tell me that a bad carpenter blames his tools.

Therein lies our answer.

***

Social media and guns are responsible for hurt, fear, risk of harm, violence and pain the world over.

You don't have to look very far for evidence of either.

The worst act of gun violence I remember from my childhood occurred in April 1999 at Columbine High School in the United States. At the time, it was the deadliest school shooting in U.S. history[5]—a record that seems morbid for me to have hoped would still stand to this day ... but sadly it does not.

This heinous act sent shockwaves through school systems all over North America. Despite being in elementary school in an entirely different country, we were told to

---

[5] https://en.wikipedia.org/wiki/Columbine_High_School_massacre.

practice active shooter drills. I'll never forget having to crawl under my desk, staring across the aisle at the huddled mass of my teacher, the look of defeat on his face as he did the same. He couldn't hold eye contact, and I prayed this was the only time I ever had to notice the pattern of scuff marks my chair had made on the classroom floor.

From the Sandy Hook massacre in 2012 to the Las Vegas shooting of 2017, guns have been at the centre of our most tragic parts of history. At the core of these violent atrocities lies an array of issues including mental health, ease of access, political unrest and, of course, war. It's not coincidental that these same issues are often intertwined with the darkest side of social media.

How far do you have to look to find the terrible side of social media? Not far when Facebook exists. Open Twitter and the vitriol floods your feed, 280 venomous characters at a time. Scroll down to the "Comments" section on any YouTube video—congratulations, you've now reached the cesspool of the internet.

But the vilest use of social media I've encountered relates back to Columbine. If you noticed above, the high-level account specifically does not mention any details about the shooters, their victims or the attack, and the reason why has now become mainstream: to discuss these perpetrators can often be construed as glorifying them. Despite the widespread use of social media coming years after the attack at Columbine, social platforms have allowed just that: the glorification of those intent on spreading hate and harm.

Fandom for the Columbine shooters emerged on sites like Tumblr. Community members even refer to themselves as "Columbiners," and they do everything from creating fan art and fan fiction, all the way down (and it really is about as far down as you can sink) to cosplaying as the pair. What's worse, this community has influenced copycats, who have drawn inspiration from the violence and attackers.

A 2014 investigation by ABC News identified "at least 17 attacks and another 36 alleged plots or serious threats against schools since the assault on Columbine High School that can be tied to the 1999 massacre."[6]

Ties that were identified included research done by copycats into the Columbine shooting, social sharing of news coverage and of Columbine images, and explicit statements of admiration of the shooters such as writings in journals and on social media in video posts. In police interviews, timing tied to an anniversary of Columbine uncovered plans to exceed the Columbine victim counts, and other vomit-inducing plans that brought me to being exactly one iota of mental resolve away from losing complete faith in us all.

In 2015, journalist Malcolm Gladwell writing in the *New Yorker* proposed a threshold model of school shootings in which the Columbine shooters were the triggering actors in "a slow-motion, ever-evolving riot, in which each new participant's action makes sense in reaction to and in combination with those who came before."[7]

Has social media aided in the spread of violence and hate by fostering communities of these like-minded individuals? I've never been more disappointed to confirm, yes, it has.

---

[6] https://abcnews.go.com/US/columbine-shootings-grim-legacy-50-school-attacks-plots/story?id=26007119.

[7] https://www.newyorker.com/magazine/2015/10/19/thresholds-of-violence.

Conducting research on this topic nearly erased all hope I had of some form of rebuttal or redemptive quality when it comes to social media until, somewhat ironically, the counterargument brought me onto social media.

Out of this horrible violence has stemmed progressive work on gun control laws, understanding high school subcultures, teenage use of pharmaceuticals, criticism of internet filters, depictions of violence in pop culture, and our ongoing war on bullying. And where do these proponents of change arise? On the exact same platforms as the Columbiners.

We cannot paint an entire walk of people with the same brush; the same can be said on social. For every twisted Tumbler (Tumblr-er? Tumblee?), there are users whose sole interest in the massacre is scholarly: to learn about the factors that caused it so we can prevent such atrocities from ever happening again.

So can a tool itself be inherently bad, or does it take human intervention to become evil? If it takes a community to sink society to new lows, then surely the reverse could also be true.

Trigger Fingers: Part II

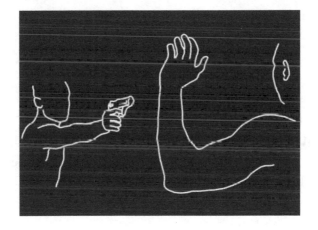

I never thought it would end like this.

He's armed, his gun pointed, and this could be the last thing I ever see or do in my life.

What previous thoughts swirled in my head, now I can't even remember.

I'm bracing for the bang.

Will it be jarring like I imagined?

I instinctively raise my hands to protect myself.

***

The single most common question I get asked to weigh in on: "Is social media bad for us?" And my answer: "It's like a gun."

Now you're probably thinking, *I read this already.* We reached the definitive conclusion that social media, like a gun, has been designed to spread hurt and harm. Case closed; you're not going to change minds. So let's then focus on changing perspectives.

Contrary to the bad carpenter who blames his tools, guns and social media, when placed in responsible hands, can be used to spread good.

***

In the blistering heat of a mid-August day in 1993, a steady hand made history.

It started when 37-year-old Doug Conley set up his plastic lawn chair in the middle of a residential intersection in Columbus, a somewhat bizarre albeit unnoteworthy act on its own, until we mention the .38-caliber revolver gripped tightly in his hands.[8]

Conley initiated a stand-off with police, shouting demands to the surrounding officers while he focused his gun on himself, the police and innocent passing drivers. He insisted on seeing his former girlfriend in between sips from a soda can that the negotiators had given him.

With the escalating situation seemingly out of control, SWAT commanders decided it was time for this to end. They called in Mike Plumb.

---

[8] https://www.dispatch.com/article/20150201/NEWS/302019879.

Mike, a Columbus SWAT sniper, had only ever fired at distant targets on the range up until that point. In fact, no Columbus police sniper in history had ever fired a shot in the line of duty, and all of that was about to change as Mike heard the word "go" come through his comms; he had the green light to put an end to this.

Plumb removed the earpiece, settled himself on the grassy hill, and watched as Conley sat straight up in his chair.

With his right hand, Doug Conley lowered the revolver between his legs—right into Plumb's crosshairs.

Bang.

Mike Plumb's shot managed to hit the gun and only the gun, shattering Conley's revolver into three pieces on the ground. The threat now neutralized and the gunman staring down in disbelief, Conley was immediately tackled by officers who handcuffed him. While being apprehended, he could be heard saying, "That was a great shot."

Mike Plumb isn't just a hero because he used his gun to save the lives of passersby and his fellow officers; he also somehow managed to save Doug's life with one brilliant sniper shot and nerves of steel.

It feels tone-deaf to highlight a protective gun story spotlighting a police officer, given both the state of distrust in the world today caused by acts of police brutality, as well as the fact that a gun protecting some often yields harm and hurt to others. Yet Mike is the perfect example of how a tool, when placed in responsible and capable hands, can help protect lives.

Much like we can draw inspiration and hope from Mike's mastery of his tool, the Red Cross has harnessed the power of social media for good of their own.

When we think of information spreading rampantly on Twitter, our minds gravitate toward a multitude of misinformation and fake news. But when Hurricane Sandy touched down on the Eastern Seaboard, the American Red Cross went digital to prevent further disaster.

Months before the hurricane hit, the Red Cross announced plans to create a Digital Operations Center: social media crisis monitoring that was set up to track online conversations. Again, we hear "track conversations" and we don't exactly throw our hands up and rejoice, but stay with me.

When the hurricane hit, social media became a vital tool for actionable intelligence for the Red Cross. During the week of Hurricane Sandy, the Red Cross tracked upward of two million posts and managed to correspond with thousands of people in need of support or information.[9]

In fact, even the lack of posting in some areas was enough to tell the Red Cross something of great consequence. Getting a teenager off their phone for a few minutes may seem like a good accomplishment in your house, but when a three-mile radius simultaneously went dark on social, they knew it was far more than good parenting or a coincidence; it meant the area probably needed help.

Clusters of people recognized the efforts of the Red Cross and began tweeting everything from "We need bottled water" to "Help, I'm not doing so well mentally." And the Red Cross responded with support.

---

[9] https:// .fastcompany.com/3020923/how-the-red-cross-used-tweets-to-save-lives-during-hurricane-sandy.

In the end, it was so effective that 88 social media posts directly affected response efforts—during Hurricane Sandy, the Red Cross's efforts on social media saved lives.

The Red Cross and Mike Plumb deserve to be recognized not only as heroes, but as proponents of change that reframe the way we should look at tools that are popular for spreading ill will. Through careful planning (and a hell of a lot of skill at their craft), these pivotal events showed us the potential of what their tools could be used for, and more people are alive today because of them.

Trigger Fingers: Part III

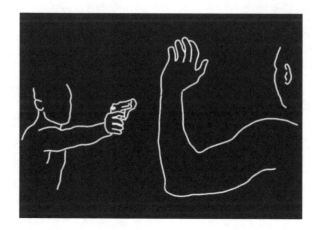

I never thought it would be like this:

I'm just the gun, a means to an end and this could be the last thing I ever do. What previous intent I had to protect is now erased by the prospect of pain, and which side I'm on I can't even remember.

I brace for the bang—

Will it be jarring like they had always imagined?

I'm focused on my target so it could end any second now.

***

By now you've likely concluded that *Trigger Fingers* is not focused on determining whether guns, like social media, are ultimately good or bad—because neither is wholly true. The analyses, like the image above, are entirely up to your interpretation. So if we can't say with certainty whether these tools are good or bad, let's instead ask: "How have they shifted the power?"

The rapid advancement of technology can be stressed in a number of ways, none more tangible than war. In World War I, soldiers rode into the battle on horses, and years later when it concluded, they flew out in airplanes.[10] Despite this monumental advancement in transportation, no single technology has changed warfare like the advent of the gun.

The earliest iterations of firearms are of interest not because they were particularly devastating, but because of how they shifted power. The earliest concept of a firearm has existed as far back as twelfth-century China in the form of a cannon-like firearm.[11] The descendent of the fire lance, it was nowhere near as sophisticated as modern weapons, but its introduction changed the battlefield.

The Yuan dynasty, a successor state to the Mongol Empire after its division and a ruling dynasty of China, was established by the infamous Kublai Khan, the leader of the Mongol Borjigin clan.[12] In 1287, their task was one common in history: defend against a rebellion, this time led by the

---

[10] https://www.ncpedia.org/wwi-technology-and-weapons-war.

[11] https://en.wikipedia.org/wiki/History_of_the_firearm.

[12] https://www.britannica.com/topic/Yuan-dynasty.

Mongol prince Nayan. How would they do this? By trying a new tactic: deploying hand cannons.

These cannons, scarcely seen before in widespread battle, not only caused damage to opposing troops in a new way they had never foreseen or planned for, but their introduction also sparked so much chaos on the battlefield that the confused enemy soldiers ended up attacking and killing each other. The rebellion was halted, and the rest is (quite literally) history—the gun had arrived, and whoever wielded it best now had a marked advantage in war.

Shifting power with our tools is not something simply buried in our history books; it still happens every day.

In 2004, a young Steve "Dangle" Glynn sat in his powder-blue childhood bedroom, with no aspirations of overthrowing an empire, his head simply filled with hockey. Despite the magnitude of his obsessive hobby, there was little reason to believe his passion would become anything more than it already was in the grand scheme of things.

Steve did not play hockey; in fact, he couldn't even skate.

Steve did not have boatloads of money to attend every game; it was a rare treat.

He had no industry connections, because he was just a kid.

And as if that wasn't enough to thwart any hope of one day working in the industry that was dominated almost exclusively by ex-players and highly decorated sports broadcasters, Steve lived in Toronto, Canada—one of the most competitive and fanatical markets in the entire hockey world.

But that never stopped him. His (now) wife bought him his first webcam, and in 2007, at the age of 19, he began posting hockey-related content to YouTube. What he's built since includes a successful series called "Leafs Fan Reactions" that has amassed over 44 million views, a continually top-trending podcast that he hosts (with our high school friend Adam Wylde), an incredible career in the industry working at Sportsnet as one of the premier hockey broadcasters in Canada and a book entitled *This Team Is Ruining My Life*—which is in part responsible for motivating me to write my own.

In 2004, YouTube was just coming into existence. Facebook was still very much in its infancy. Twitter? Didn't even exist yet. So three of the most powerful tools that Steve would use in his arsenal to go from obscurity to one of the most-loved hockey personalities the world over were completely unbeknownst to most. Steve shifted power by establishing voice, presence and community. He is the epitome of what an influencer should strive to be, not because he's successful, but because when the red light goes off, Steve goes back to being the great person he's always been.

He's since learned to skate. Not only does he now get to attend many Maple Leafs games, but he's also in the locker room talking to the players; many of them are fans and watch his videos. And if it weren't for the experiences he's shared and the guidance he's provided, I never would have known where to start with *Trigger Fingers*.

With the age of the internet, influencers took the seemingly hopeless state of one-way broadcast media and flipped it on its head through social media. As we've discussed in previous chapters, sometimes this power in the wrong hands can be used to cause pain, but often social media has provided a voice to the voiceless. With that voice, power shifts. Much like on the battlefield, it incites chaos, sparks confusion and calls into question whether this is the innovation that will propel us forward or destroy us all.

I, for one, see these tools as just that: neither good nor evil, simply there for the taking, ready to be wielded by those with a microphone and a message. I'm so excited to see the tools of tomorrow picked up by the next Steve Dangle in their powder-blue bedroom, with nothing but passion and a purpose.

What's yours?

Acknowledgements

Writing a book quite literally takes a small army, and the only battles I had commanded prior to *Trigger Fingers* consisted of a plunger and an unruly toilet.

I want to thank my mother, Janice, for encouraging me to cultivate the wildest of imaginations as a child, and for never forcing me to truly grow up. I write of superheroes so vividly because I stood witness to one at home.

I am eternally indebted to my wife, Amberlie, my rock, who listened to my endless droning on about this book and never once ran away, despite being trapped in our shoebox of an apartment during the height of a global pandemic. Everything I do, I do for you.

To my best friends Omey and Dave, the latter being the first person to ever add fuel to the fire of writing a book: you may not know it from these pages, but many of the anecdotes enclosed are shared stories that I will forever cherish having experienced them with the best lifelong friends a guy could ask for.

To my loving family who have always supported me and dared me to dream bigger, thank you for always being in my corner.

Thank you to my industry peers Hamza Khan and Luki Danukarjanto, for sharing your advice from the perspective of a published author and for being so giving of your time when I wasn't sure how to string more than two sentences together.

To my masterful artists, aksaramantra and Mike Tommasone, thank you for being so generous with your talent and time, and for bringing the imagery of this book to life.

To my editor and guardian angel Johanna Petronella Leigh, words cannot describe the gratitude I should express for all you've done for me. I trusted you with my words and you have given me so much more in return.

To Tom Corson-Knowles, for challenging me to take this book from a glorified pamphlet to something that I'd be proud to share, your mentoring and sage advice have only made me want to work with you that much more in the future; thank you.

To my publishers at Iguana, for being the very first publisher to believe in me and never wavering in that support. Before you, I wasn't sure if this would simply stay a .PDF I would email to friends, colleagues and students. Thank you for helping me accomplish a lifelong goal.

To Steve "Dangle" Glynn, for taking the extra long route while you walked your dog Iggy in the dead of winter, just so you could stay on the phone with me a little longer and tell me exactly what I needed to do to produce a book of my own. With each passing day, I am even more proud of you, my friend.

And finally, to my aunt Karen Rodricks, for placing a book under the tree at Christmas in 1997 which would inspire a lifelong infatuation with reading, writing and storytelling.

> *"Clear eyes, full hearts, can't lose."*
> —Coach Taylor, *Friday Night Lights*

About the Author

Adam Rodricks is an international-award-winning social media strategist and speaker who has transformed "word of mouth" into a world of mouth for Fortune 500 companies. In 2020, he was named "Canada's Top Social Media Strategist" by the Speakers Bureau of Canada.

His speaking career, where he has been featured on some of the world's largest stages, most notably at Collision

Conference in 2021, served as the catalyst for this book. Adam also teaches the LinkedIn Fundamentals course at a local Toronto college and serves on the Program Advisory Board for Digital Engagement Strategy for another post-secondary institution in Ontario.

His work as a social media influencer has been featured on CBC, CTV, Yahoo, BNN, DigitalJournal.com, Maximum PC, Nintendo.ca and his own site, adamrodricks.com.